VOLUME TWO

# THE
# R·U·L·E·S
# *of*
# ENGAGEMENT

## BINDING THE STRONGMAN

# DR. N. CINDY TRIMM

CREATION HOUSE
A STRANG COMPANY

THE RULES OF ENGAGEMENT, VOL. 2:
BINDING THE STRONGMAN by Dr. N. Cindy Trimm
Published by Creation House
A Strang Company
600 Rinehart Road
Lake Mary, Florida 32746
www.creationhouse.com

Unless otherwise noted, all Scripture quotations are from the King James Version of the Bible.

Scripture quotations marked TLB are from The Living Bible. Copyright © 1971. Used by permission of Tyndale House Publishers, Inc., Wheaton, IL 60189. All rights reserved.

Publisher's note: this book is not intended to provide medical advice or to take the place of medical advice treatment from your personal physician. Readers are advised to consult their own doctors or other qualified health professionals regarding the treatment of their medical conditions. Neither the publisher nor the author takes any responsibility for any possible consequences from following the information in this book.

Cover design by Terry Clifton

Library of Congress Control Number: 2005927879
International Standard Book Number: 978-1-59185-822-5
First Edition
07 08 09 10—9 8 7 6 5 4
Printed in the United States of America

# Contents

# Introduction

THE BIBLE CLEARLY states that the purpose for which Christ was born was to destroy the works of Satan. We know that Christ completed His mission on the cross. Scripture clearly states that Christ's job description was the exact antithesis of the enemy's. According to John 10:10, Christ came to bring life, but Satan came "to steal, and to kill, and to destroy." He is relentless in his attempts to undermine the plans and purposes of God. He is skillful at even disguising himself so as to remain undetected. As believers, we need not be afraid, but be aware and empowered to have the ability to identify the works of the enemy, and understand that God has given us His power to tread on serpents, scorpions, and over all the power of the enemy so that according to Luke 10:19, "nothing shall by any means hurt you [us]."

The time has come when God has stirred up the hearts of all believers to rise up and take their rightful places as His official representatives in the earthly realm. Our role is to activate and enforce the authority God has given us.

As an empowered believer, you should no longer be satisfied with standing on the sidelines, accepting anything from the enemy as if that stance is acceptable. There is a real battle going on. We have a real enemy. There are no demilitarized zones in this battle. Thank God we have been given the assurance that, in this warfare, we are fighting the good fight of faith. The outcome has been decided, and our victory has been downloaded into the equation.

I have never seen an age like this, where there is such a desire to see souls saved and the church filled with the glory of God. God is birthing His plans in every nation and amongst all peoples. The kingdom of heaven is prevailing as the end of the age quickly approaches. We are getting ready for the final showdown: when the saints of God will deliver the final blow to the enemy and deliver the kingdoms of this world to Him. We will not only "bind the strongman," but we will also render him hopelessly helpless to prevent the next move of God in our personal lives, churches, ministries, communities, and nations.

Kingdom Life Publishing is expanding at an astounding rate, offering books with empowering messages that lead their readers to maximizing their potential. We offer a variety of books and biblical courses written by the author for all levels of study. As part of our Prayer Series, *The Rules of Engagement, Vol. 2: Binding the Strongman* offers much to readers who want to learn more about the power of strategic prayers. Refer to the preceding book, *The Rules of Engagement, Vol. 1: The Art of Strategic Prayer and Spiritual Warfare*, which offers practical, revolutionary insights and compelling biblical commentary geared toward equipping generals of prayer. This series will take your prayer life to another level as you are divinely empowered to:

- Assess situations and circumstances accurately based on spiritual laws and principles

- Recognize and identify the presence and activities of principalities and their subordinate spirits

- Sever the root causes of satanic influences and demonic activities

- Gain and maintain spiritual authority over regions and territories

- Gain and regain control over your life and relationships.

*Binding the Strongman* is by no means an exhaustive commentary. Instead, it was written with the intention of being used as a handy, user-friendly, easy-to-read reference book. By utilizing powerful, practical tools and insights designed to give you victory in all your battles, you will be divinely empowered to effectively penetrate and plunder the kingdom of darkness, while promoting and populating the kingdom of heaven. Let the earth resound in concert with the heavenly hosts, saying, "The kingdoms of this world are become the kingdoms of our Lord, and of his Christ; and he shall reign forever and ever" (Rev. 11:15).

## How to Use This Book

By effectively utilizing this powerful, practical tool you will gain a biblically-based insight into the nature of spirits. After thoroughly acquainting yourself with the Introduction and Chapter 1, I suggest that you begin at the back of the book. You will notice the index is alphabetized for ease of reference. Determine the spirit you are fighting. You will notice capitalized words in brackets. The capitalized words are the strongman, or dominant spirits, and the lowercased words are the subordinate spirits. You will also notice that more than one strongman can utilize one subordinate spirit, or they may even act as a strongmen to other spirits. One reason many people do not experience the kind of success they want when engaging in this type of warfare is generalization or ignorance. Do not fall into the trap of making a sweeping generalization, and do not war ignorantly. This book is designed to unveil the hidden truths about how spirits are so masterful in their warfare. They engineer many deceptive activities that sometimes could fool the most skilled spiritual warrior. Your reliance is upon the Lord and not your skill. Therefore, as you engage in warfare, it is important to wipe out all associated spirits. Once you identify the subordinate spirits and the strongman, go to the front of the book, and identify the page that the strongman and subordinate spirits are detailed. Apprise yourself of the unique characteristics of the strongman. Cover yourself with the armor of the Lord, and begin to bind and loose, utilizing the authority of Jesus' name. Ask God to bring total deliverance to that person, city, ministry, or nation.

This book has been designed to give you victory in all your battles and to divinely empower you to penetrate and plunder the kingdom of darkness while promoting and populating the kingdom of heaven. Let the earth resound in concert with the heavenly hosts.

Please allow this book to empower you with truth and equip you with powerful weapons of warfare as you give this manual your undivided attention. Let the Holy Spirit reveal to you the truth. Anticipate this truth not only liberating you but everything and everyone associated with you in Jesus' name.

# Understanding the Kingdom of Darkness

NEW STUDENTS OF the Bible, and even veterans with firm spiritual foundations and studies, often wonder about this figure called Satan. Is Satan a literal being? Is hell a literal place? Is there really a kingdom of darkness? By thoroughly studying the Word of God you will acquire a greater understanding of Satan and his kingdom, thus eliminating ignorance, which is one of his greatest weapons.

## There Are Two Kingdoms Mentioned in the Bible

The line on the battlefield has been drawn between the kingdom of darkness and the kingdom of light. Every individual must choose one side or the other. As believers, thank God we have been delivered from the authorities that rule in the kingdom of darkness. God has restored to us the dominion originally given to man in the Garden of Eden. God has ordained that even as Christ is the Head of the church and the church is His body, we are assured of victory over every demonic force in Jesus' name. "And his reason? To show to all the rulers [principalities and powers] in heaven how perfectly wise he is when all of his family—Jews and Gentiles alike—are seen to be joined together in his Church in just the way he had always planned it through Jesus Christ our Lord" (Eph. 3:10–11, TLB).

> Who hath delivered us from the power of darkness, and hath translated us into the kingdom of his dear Son.
>
> —COLOSSIANS 1:13

> Now thanks be unto God, which always causeth us to triumph in Christ, and maketh manifest the saviour of his knowledge by us in every place.
>
> —2 CORINTHIANS 2:14

## The Kingdom of Darkness Is a Literal, Spiritual Kingdom

Think of the kingdom of darkness as you would any other earthly, terrestrial nation or country. However, there is one difference; that difference lies in its essence. Essentially the kingdom of darkness, although literal, is not physical, but spiritual in nature. The following texts will give you more insight and revelation:

> And after these things I saw another angel come down from heaven, having great power; and the earth was lightened with his glory. And he cried mightily with a strong voice, saying, Babylon the

great is fallen, is fallen, and is become the habitation
of devils, and the hold of every foul spirit, and a cage
of every unclean and hateful bird. For all nations
have drunk of the wine of the wrath of her fornication, and the kings of the earth have committed
fornication with her, and the merchants of the earth
are waxed rich through the abundance of her delicacies. And I heard another voice from heaven, saying,
Come out of her, my people, that ye be not partakers
of her sins, and that ye receive not of her plagues.
For her sins have reached unto heaven, and God
hath remembered her iniquities. Reward her even
as she rewarded you, and double unto her double
according to her works: in the cup which she hath
filled fill to her double. How much she hath glorified herself, and lived deliciously, so much torment
and sorrow give her: for she saith in her heart, I sit
a queen, and am no widow, and shall see no sorrow.
Therefore shall her plagues come in one day, death,
and mourning, and famine; and she shall be utterly
burned with fire: for strong is the Lord God who
judgeth her. And the kings of the earth, who have
committed fornication and lived deliciously with
her, shall bewail her, and lament for her, when they
shall see the smoke of her burning, Standing afar off
for the fear of her torment, saying, Alas, alas that
great city Babylon, that mighty city! for in one hour
is thy judgment come. And the merchants of the
earth shall weep and mourn over her; for no man
buyeth their merchandise any more: The merchandise of gold, and silver, and precious stones, and of
pearls, and fine linen, and purple, and silk, and scarlet, and all thyine wood, and all manner vessels of

ivory, and all manner vessels of most precious wood, and of brass, and iron, and marble, And cinnamon, and odours, and ointments, and frankincense, and wine, and oil, and fine flour, and wheat, and beasts, and sheep, and horses, and chariots, and slaves, and souls of men. And the fruits that thy soul lusted after are departed from thee, and all things which were dainty and goodly are departed from thee, and thou shalt find them no more at all. The merchants of these things, which were made rich by her, shall stand afar off for the fear of her torment, weeping and wailing, And saying, Alas, alas, that great city, that was clothed in fine linen, and purple, and scarlet, and decked with gold, and precious stones, and pearls! For in one hour so great riches is come to nought. And every shipmaster, and all the company in ships, and sailors, and as many as trade by sea, stood afar off, And cried when they saw the smoke of her burning, saying, What city is like unto this great city! And they cast dust on their heads, and cried, weeping and wailing, saying, Alas, alas, that great city, wherein were made rich all that had ships in the sea by reason of her costliness! for in one hour is she made desolate. Rejoice over her, thou heaven, and ye holy apostles and prophets; for God hath avenged you on her. And a mighty angel took up a stone like a great millstone, and cast it into the sea, saying, Thus with violence shall that great city Babylon be thrown down, and shall be found no more at all. And the voice of harpers, and musicians, and of pipers, and trumpeters, shall be heard no more at all in thee; and no craftsman, of whatsoever craft he be, shall be found any more in thee; and the sound

of a millstone shall be heard no more at all in thee;
And the light of a candle shall shine no more at all
in thee; and the voice of the bridegroom and of the
bride shall be heard no more at all in thee: for thy
merchants were the great men of the earth; for by
thy sorceries were all nations deceived. And in her
was found the blood of prophets, and of saints, and
of all that were slain upon the earth.

—REVELATION 18:1–24

And the angels which kept not their first estate, but
left their own habitation, he hath reserved in everlasting chains under darkness unto the judgment of
the great day.

—JUDE 1:6

And the fourth angel poured out his vial upon the
sun; and power was given unto him to scorch men
with fire. And men were scorched with great heat,
and blasphemed the name of God, which hath
power over these plagues: and they repented not to
give him glory. And the fifth angel poured out his
vial upon the seat of the beast; and his kingdom was
full of darkness; and they gnawed their tongues for
pain, And blasphemed the God of heaven because of
their pains and their sores, and repented not of their
deeds. And the sixth angel poured out his vial upon
the great river Euphrates; and the water thereof was
dried up, that the way of the kings of the east might
be prepared. And I saw three unclean spirits like
frogs come out of the mouth of the dragon, and out
of the mouth of the beast, and out of the mouth of
the false prophet. For they are the spirits of devils,

working miracles, which go forth unto the kings of the earth and of the whole world, to gather them to the battle of that great day of God Almighty.

—REVELATION 16:8–14

There are several things you must know about the kingdom of darkness:

### *It was instituted by Satan and a host of fallen angels.*

The Bible tells how this kingdom of darkness was created. Having seduced approximately one-third of the angelic host, Satan proceeded to organize a foiled insurrection that subsequently led to their expulsion from heaven. What an event! Jesus describes it as a light show in the heavens:

And he said unto them, I beheld Satan as lightning fall from heaven.

—LUKE 10:18

And there appeared another wonder in heaven; and behold a great red dragon, having seven heads and ten horns, and seven crowns upon his heads. And his tail drew the third part of the stars of heaven, and did cast them to the earth: and the dragon stood before the woman which was ready to be delivered, for to devour her child as soon as it was born. And she brought forth a man child, who was to rule all nations with a rod of iron: and her child was caught up unto God, and to his throne. And the woman fled into the wilderness, where she hath a place prepared of God, that they should feed her there a thousand two hundred and threescore days. And there was war in heaven: Michael and his angels fought against the dragon; and the dragon fought and his angels, And prevailed not; neither was their place found any more in heaven. And the great dragon was cast out, that old serpent, called the Devil, and Satan, which deceiveth the whole world: he was cast out into the earth, and his angels were cast out with him. And I heard a loud voice saying in heaven, Now is come salvation, and strength, and the kingdom of our God, and the power of his Christ: for the accuser of our brethren is cast down, which accused them before our God day and night. And they overcame him by the blood of the Lamb, and by the word of their testimony; and they loved not their lives unto the death. Therefore rejoice, ye heavens, and ye that dwell in them. Woe to the inhabiters of the earth and of the sea! for the devil is come down unto you, having great wrath, because he knoweth that he hath but a short time. And when the dragon saw that he was cast unto the earth, he persecuted the woman which brought forth the man child.

—REVELATION 12:3–13

### *This satanic kingdom has a cosmological system.*

The word *cosmology* speaks of the dynamic arrangement of the universe and the world. God created the world in an orderly fashion. Satan has created a perverted imitation of it. By using such people as Cain and other rebellious men as pawns, he has successfully constructed a world that in reality is nothing more than just a great magic show with illusions, smoke, and mirrors to fool the blinded eyes of man. Although illusory in nature, Satan has succeeded in creating a well-organized system of evil:

And the LORD said unto Cain, Where is Abel thy brother? And he said, I know not: Am I my brother's keeper? And he said, What hast thou done? the voice of thy brother's blood crieth unto me from the ground. And now art thou cursed from the earth, which hath opened her mouth to receive thy brother's blood from thy hand; When thou tillest the ground, it shall not henceforth yield unto thee her strength; a fugitive and a vagabond shalt thou be in the earth. And Cain said unto the LORD, My punishment is greater than I can bear. Behold, thou hast driven me out this day from the face of the earth; and from thy face shall I be hid; and I shall be a fugitive and a vagabond in the earth; and it shall come to pass, that every one that findeth me shall slay me. And the LORD said unto him, Therefore whosoever slayeth Cain, vengeance shall be taken on him sevenfold. And the LORD set a mark upon Cain, lest any finding him should kill him. And Cain went out from the presence of the LORD, and dwelt in the land of Nod, on the east of Eden. And Cain knew his wife; and she conceived, and bare Enoch: and he builded a city, and called the name of the city, after the name of his son, Enoch. And unto Enoch was born Irad: and Irad begat Mehujael: and Mehujael begat Methusael: and Methusael begat Lamech. And Lamech took unto him two wives: the name of the one was Adah, and the name of the other Zillah. And Adah bare Jabal: he was the father of such as dwell in tents, and of such as have cattle. And his brother's name was Jubal: he was the father of all such as handle the harp and organ. And Zillah, she also bare Tubal-cain, an instructer of every artificer in brass and iron: and the sister of Tubal-cain was Naamah. And Lamech said unto his wives, Adah and Zillah, Hear my voice; ye wives of Lamech, hearken unto my speech: for I have slain a man to my wounding, and a young man to my hurt. If Cain shall be avenged sevenfold, truly Lamech seventy and sevenfold.

—GENESIS 4:9–24

In this particular text we see the terrestrial foundation of the kingdom of darkness taking shape and form through the creation of eight out of the twelve existing systems that comprise our world:

- Social System (e.g: culture, entertainment, language, marriage, or family)
- Entertainment
- Environmental
- Economic
- Governmental
- Educational
- Technological
- Religious (humanistic, atheistic, and anti-God)

These systems, originally designed by God to provide the optimum environment for mankind to fulfill purpose, maximize potential, and reach destiny, have not become the strongholds of demonic forces. Today we can witness the effects of the presence of the enemy in this world. Governments are corrupt, one in every two marriages ends in divorce, families that once were safe havens for children are now plagued with abuse and domestic violence, leaving the educational institution wanting. Satan eroded and corroded the foundation and fiber of societies and institutions creating the bedrock for sin and iniquity to be perpetuated intergenerationally.

> And the kings of the earth, who have committed fornication and lived deliciously with her, shall bewail her, and lament for her, when they shall see the smoke of her burning, Standing afar off for the fear of her torment, saying, Alas, alas that great city Babylon, that mighty city! for in one hour is thy judgment come.... And the light of a candle shall shine no more at all in thee; and the voice of the bridegroom and of the bride shall be heard no more at all in thee: for thy merchants were the great men of the earth; for by thy sorceries were all nations deceived. And in her was found the blood of prophets, and of saints, and of all that were slain upon the earth.

> —REVELATION 18:9–10, 23–24

And it came to pass, when men began to multiply on the face of the earth, and daughters were born unto them, That the sons of God saw the daughters of men that they were fair; and they took them wives of all which they chose. And the LORD said, My spirit shall not always strive with man, for that he also is flesh: yet his days shall be an hundred and twenty years. There were giants in the earth in those days; and also after that, when the sons of God came in unto the daughters of men, and they bare children to them, the same became mighty men which were of old, men of renown. And God saw that the wickedness of man was great in the earth, and that every imagination of the thoughts of his heart was only evil continually. And it repented the LORD that he had made man on the earth, and it grieved him at his heart. And the LORD said, I will destroy man whom I have created from the face of the earth; both man, and beast, and the creeping thing, and the fowls of the air; for it repenteth me that I have made them.

—GENESIS 6:1–7

*Although Satan is his kingdom's principal leader, God has given us authority and power to expose his tactics and overcome his attack.*

Satan rules the kingdom of darkness. Remember, he is the prince of the power of the air, and not the earth. Man has been given dominion over the earth realm. (See Genesis 1:28; Psalm 115:15–16.) His activities are illegal because disembodied spirits were not given authority to operate on the earth. This is why Satan had to possess the body of a snake in order to gain legal access. Possession is his current strategy for control in the earth realm. He knew the law of undertaking any initiatives in the earth realm. Flesh and blood is the spiritual protocol for operating here, a protocol which even God subjects Himself to. When God wanted to redeem the world, He came in the form of the flesh through Jesus Christ our Lord: our Leader, the King of kings, the Lord of lords, the commanding Officer of the heavenly hosts, our General and mighty Man of war who has given you authority over all the power of the enemy. It is up to you and me to enforce that authority.

Wherein in time past ye walked according to the course of this world, according to the prince of the

power of the air, the spirit that now worketh in the
children of disobedience.

—EPHESIANS 2:2

The heaven, even the heavens, are the LORD's: but
the earth hath he given to the children of men.

—PSALM 115:16

What is man, that thou art mindful of him? and the
son of man, that thou visitest him? For thou hast
made him a little lower than the angels, and hast
crowned him with glory and honour. Thou madest
him to have dominion over the works of thy hands;
thou hast put all things under his feet.

—PSALM 8:4–6

Behold, I give unto you power to tread on serpents
and scorpions, and over all the power of the enemy:
and nothing shall by any means hurt you.

—LUKE 10:19

Satan has set himself up to be as god in the earth
realm. He is an imposter and an impersonator. Since
God aborted his diabolical *coup d'état* (aggressive take-
over) in the third heavens, he now attempts to become
a god over the inhabitants of the earth. You must put up
a resistance.

How art thou fallen from heaven, O Lucifer, son of
the morning! how art thou cut down to the ground,
which didst weaken the nations! For thou hast said
in thine heart, I will ascend into heaven, I will exalt
my throne above the stars of God: I will sit also
upon the mount of the congregation, in the sides

of the north: I will ascend above the heights of the clouds; I will be like the most High.

—ISAIAH 14:12–14

Submit yourselves therefore to God. Resist the devil, and he will flee from you.

—JAMES 4:7

*Satan and his demonic cohorts have the ability to oppress, possess, and terrorize humanity.*

You must identify the spirits, take your authority over the enemy, and bind their activities in Jesus' name. You will learn more about this as you proceed through this book.

Yet thou shalt be brought down to hell, to the sides of the pit. They that see thee shall narrowly look upon thee, and consider thee, saying, Is this the man that made the earth to tremble, that did shake kingdoms; That made the world as a wilderness, and destroyed the cities thereof; that opened not the house of his prisoners? All the kings of the nations, even all of them, lie in glory, every one in his own house. But thou art cast out of thy grave like an abominable branch, and as the raiment of those that are slain, thrust through with a sword, that go down to the stones of the pit; as a carcase trodden under feet. Thou shalt not be joined with them in burial, because thou hast destroyed thy land, and slain thy people: the seed of evildoers shall never be renowned. Prepare slaughter for his children for the iniquity of their fathers; that they do not rise, nor possess the land, nor fill the face of the world with cities.

—ISAIAH 14:15–21

And there was war in heaven: Michael and his angels fought against the dragon; and the dragon fought and his angels, And prevailed not; neither was their place found any more in heaven. And the great dragon was cast out, that old serpent, called the Devil, and Satan, which deceiveth the whole world: he was cast out into the earth, and his angels were cast out with him. And I heard a loud voice saying in heaven, Now is come salvation, and strength, and the kingdom of our God, and the power of his Christ: for the accuser of our brethren is cast down, which accused them before our God day and night. And they overcame him by the blood of the Lamb, and by the word of their testimony; and they loved not their lives unto the death. Therefore rejoice, ye heavens, and ye that dwell in them. Woe to the inhabiters of the earth and of the sea! for the devil is come down unto you, having great wrath, because he knoweth that he hath but a short time. And when the dragon saw that he was cast unto the earth, he persecuted the woman which brought forth the man child.

—Revelation 12:7–13

No man can enter into a strong man's house, and spoil his goods, except he will first bind the strong man; and then he will spoil his house.

—Mark 3:27

And he shall speak great words against the most High, and shall wear out the saints of the most High, and think to change times and laws: and they shall be given into his hand until a time and times and the dividing of time. But the judgment shall sit, and they shall take away his dominion, to consume and to destroy it unto the end. And the kingdom and dominion, and the greatness of the kingdom under the whole heaven, shall be given to the people of the saints of the most High, whose kingdom is an everlasting kingdom, and all dominions shall serve and obey him.

—DANIEL 7:25–27

### This kingdom of darkness has a sophisticated economy.

As with any other earthly kingdom, it trades and transacts business. Satan has built an entire evil empire by utilizing the most precious of all commodities, intellectual properties, and the very souls of men. When it comes to humanity, many people have replaced their love of God with the love of money. First Timothy 6:10 declares, "For the love of money is the root of all evil: which while some coveted after, they have erred from the faith, and pierced themselves through with many sorrows." Throughout history we can trace many atrocities, sinful, unholy, and ungodly activities, to this inordinate affection and idolatrous stronghold in the minds of men. Like the black widow spider that lures her prey into its web and to its demise, this satanic economic system will lure any and every soul it can into a web designed for death and destruction.

And the merchants of the earth shall weep and mourn over her; for no man buyeth their merchandise any more: The merchandise of gold, and silver, and precious stones, and of pearls, and fine linen, and purple, and silk, and scarlet, and all thyine wood, and all manner vessels of ivory, and all manner vessels of most precious wood, and of brass, and iron, and marble, And cinnamon, and odours, and ointments, and frankincense, and wine, and oil, and fine flour, and wheat, and beasts, and sheep, and horses, and chariots, and slaves, and souls of men. And the fruits that thy soul lusted after are departed from thee, and all things which were dainty and goodly are departed from thee, and thou shalt find them no more at all. The merchants of these things, which were made rich by her, shall stand afar off for the fear of her torment, weeping and wailing, And saying, Alas, alas, that great city, that was clothed in fine linen, and purple, and scarlet, and decked with gold, and precious stones, and pearls! For in one hour so great riches is come to nought. And every shipmaster, and all the company in ships, and sailors, and as many as trade by sea, stood afar off, And cried when they saw the smoke of her burning, saying, What city is like unto this great city! And they cast dust on their heads, and cried, weeping and wailing, saying, Alas, alas, that great city, wherein were made rich all that had ships in the sea by reason of her costliness! for in one hour is she made desolate. Rejoice over her, thou heaven, and ye holy apostles and prophets; for God hath avenged you on her. And a mighty angel took up a stone like a great millstone, and cast it into the sea, saying, Thus with violence shall that great city Babylon be thrown down, and shall be found no more at all. And the voice of harpers, and musicians, and of pipers, and trumpeters, shall be heard no more at

all in thee; and no craftsman, of whatsoever craft he
be, shall be found any more in thee; and the sound
of a millstone shall be heard no more at all in thee.
—REVELATION 18:11–22

Now, thou son of man, take up a lamentation for
Tyrus; And say unto Tyrus, O thou that art situate at
the entry of the sea, which art a merchant of the people for many isles, Thus saith the Lord GOD; O Tyrus,
thou hast said, I am of perfect beauty. Thy borders are
in the midst of the seas, thy builders have perfected
thy beauty. They have made all thy ship boards of fir
trees of Senir: they have taken cedars from Lebanon
to make masts for thee. Of the oaks of Bashan have
they made thine oars; the company of the Ashurites
have made thy benches of ivory, brought out of the
isles of Chittim. Fine linen with broidered work from
Egypt was that which thou spreadest forth to be thy
sail; blue and purple from the isles of Elishah was
that which covered thee. The inhabitants of Zidon
and Arvad were thy mariners: thy wise men, O
Tyrus, that were in thee, were thy pilots. The ancients
of Gebal and the wise men thereof were in thee thy
calkers: and all the ships of the sea with their mariners were in thee to occupy thy merchandise. They
of Persia and of Lud and of Phut were in thine army,
thy men of war: they hanged the shield and helmet
in thee; they set forth thy comeliness. The men of
Arvad with thine army were upon thy walls round
about, and the Gammadims were in thy towers: they
hanged their shields upon thy walls round about;
they have made thy beauty perfect. Tarshish was thy
merchant by reason of the multitude of all kind of

riches; with silver, iron, tin, and lead, they traded in thy fairs. Javan, Tubal, and Meshech, they were thy merchants: they traded the persons of men and vessels of brass in thy market. They of the house of Togarmah traded in thy fairs with horses and horsemen and mules. The men of Dedan were thy merchants; many isles were the merchandise of thine hand: they brought thee for a present horns of ivory and ebony. Syria was thy merchant by reason of the multitude of the wares of thy making: they occupied in thy fairs with emeralds, purple, and broidered work, and fine linen, and coral, and agate. Judah, and the land of Israel, they were thy merchants: they traded in thy market wheat of Minnith, and Pannag, and honey, and oil, and balm. Damascus was thy merchant in the multitude of the wares of thy making, for the multitude of all riches; in the wine of Helbon, and white wool. Dan also and Javan going to and fro occupied in thy fairs: bright iron, cassia, and calamus, were in thy market. Dedan was thy merchant in precious clothes for chariots. Arabia, and all the princes of Kedar, they occupied with thee in lambs, and rams, and goats: in these were they thy merchants. The merchants of Sheba and Raamah, they were thy merchants: they occupied in thy fairs with chief of all spices, and with all precious stones, and gold. Haran, and Canneh, and Eden, the merchants of Sheba, Assur, and Chilmad, were thy merchants. These were thy merchants in all sorts of things, in blue clothes, and broidered work, and in chests of rich apparel, bound with cords, and made of cedar, among thy merchandise. The ships of Tarshish did sing of thee in thy market: and thou wast replenished, and made very glorious in the midst of the seas. Thy rowers have brought thee into great waters: the east wind hath broken thee in the midst of the seas.

—EZEKIEL 27:2–26

### *The kingdom of Satan is a kingdom of darkness.*

When we speak of the kingdom of darkness we speak of any territory or domain where there is an absence of God, revelation, divine purpose, and destiny. Spiritual blindness is another weapon of mass destruction. In short, this is an effective weapon because, even if truth is presented, the blinded cannot see unless there is divine intervention through salvation, healing, and deliverance. The Living Bible gives us the reason for this level of spiritual blindness in 2 Corinthians 4:4, which lets us know that, "Satan, who is the god of this evil world, has made them blind, unable to see the glorious light of the Gospel that is shining upon him or to understand the amazing message we preach about the glory of Christ, who is God" (TLB).

And the earth was without form, and void; and darkness was upon the face of the deep. And the Spirit of God moved upon the face of the waters. And God said, Let there be light: and there was light. And God saw the light, that it was good: and God divided the light from the darkness.

—GENESIS 1:2–4

And thou shalt grope at noonday, as the blind gropeth in darkness, and thou shalt not prosper in thy ways: and thou shalt be only oppressed and spoiled evermore, and no man shall save thee.

—DEUTERONOMY 28:29

They grope in the dark without light, and he maketh them to stagger like a drunken man [with no direction, hope or understanding of purpose and will of God for their lives].

—JOB 12:25 (AUTHOR'S PARAPHRASE)

We grope for the wall like the blind, and we grope as if we had no eyes: we stumble at noonday as in the night; we are in desolate places as dead men.

—ISAIAH 59:10

***The kingdom of darkness is accessible to both spirit beings and human beings who either visit or make their abode there.***

Fallen angels dwell there. This kingdom of darkness is not far removed from us at all. As human beings, we can abandon the laws of God—the laws that would bring us the peace that surpasses all understanding—and live in the kingdom of darkness as well. In the following text the Bible speaks of Babylon. Babylon is to the kingdom of darkness as Washington DC is to the United States, or London is to England. Think of it as you would the capital of your country:

And after these things I saw another angel come down from heaven, having great power; and the earth was lightened with his glory. And he cried mightily with a strong voice, saying, Babylon the great is fallen, is fallen, and is become the habitation of devils, and the hold of every foul spirit, and a cage of every unclean and hateful bird. For all nations have drunk of the wine of the wrath of her fornication, and the kings of the earth have committed fornication with her, and the merchants of the earth are waxed rich through the abundance of her delicacies. And I heard another voice from heaven, saying, Come out of her, my people, that ye be not partakers of her sins, and that ye receive not of her plagues.

—REVELATION 18:1–4

And the angels which kept not their first estate, but left their own habitation, he hath reserved in everlasting chains under darkness unto the judgment of the great day.

—JUDE 1:6

And after these things I saw another angel come down from heaven, having great power; and the earth was lightened with his glory. And he cried mightily with a strong voice, saying, Babylon the great is fallen, is fallen, and is become the habitation of devils, and the hold of every foul spirit, and a cage of every unclean and hateful bird.

—REVELATION 18:1–2

*Like our own worship of the Lord our God, the kingdom of darkness also has a mode of worship.*

Just as your worship brings you into the presence of God, satanic worship will bring you into the presence of Satan. Remember, worship is not just an activity in a church or synagogue; it is the lifestyle you choose to live on a daily basis. The question that I pose to you today is, "Does your life bring glory to God or to Satan?"

And there came one of the seven angels which had the seven vials, and talked with me, saying unto me, Come hither; I will shew unto thee the judgment of the great whore that sitteth upon many waters: With whom the kings of the earth have committed fornication, and the inhabitants of the earth have been made drunk with the wine of her fornication. So he carried me away in the spirit into the wilderness: and I saw a woman sit upon a scarlet coloured beast, full of names of blasphemy, having seven heads and ten horns. And the woman was arrayed in purple and scarlet colour, and decked with gold and precious stones and pearls, having a golden cup in her hand full of abominations and filthiness of her fornication: and upon her forehead was a name written, MYSTERY, BABYLON THE GREAT, THE MOTHER OF HARLOTS AND ABOMINATIONS OF THE EARTH. And I saw the woman drunken with the blood of the saints, and with the blood of the martyrs of Jesus: and when I saw her, I wondered with great admiration.

—REVELATION 17:1–6

Nebuchadnezzar the king made an image of gold, whose height was threescore cubits, and the breadth thereof six cubits: he set it up in the plain of Dura, in the province of Babylon. Then Nebuchadnezzar the king sent to gather together the princes, the governors, and the captains, the judges, the treasurers, the counsellors, the sheriffs, and all the rulers of the provinces, to come to the dedication of the image which Nebuchadnezzar the king had set up. Then the princes, the governors, and captains, the judges, the treasurers, the counsellors, the sheriffs, and all the rulers of the provinces, were gathered together unto the dedication of the image that Nebuchadnezzar the king had set up; and they stood before the image that Nebuchadnezzar had set up. Then an herald cried aloud, To you it is commanded, O people, nations, and languages, That at what time ye hear the sound of the cornet, flute, harp, sackbut, psaltery, dulcimer, and all kinds of musick, ye fall down and worship the golden image that Nebuchadnezzar the king hath set up: And whoso falleth not down and worshippeth shall the same hour be cast into the midst of a burning fiery furnace. Therefore at that time, when all the people heard the sound of the cornet, flute, harp, sackbut, psaltery, and all kinds of musick, all the people, the nations, and the languages, fell down and worshipped the golden image that Nebuchadnezzar the king had set up. Wherefore at that time certain Chaldeans came near, and accused the Jews. They spake and said to the king Nebuchadnezzar, O king, live for ever. Thou, O king, hast made a decree, that every man that shall hear the sound of the cornet, flute, harp, sackbut, psaltery, and dulcimer, and all kinds of musick, shall fall down and worship the golden image: And whoso falleth not down and worshippeth, that he should be cast into the midst of a burning fiery furnace. There are certain Jews whom thou hast set over the affairs of the province of Babylon, Shadrach, Meshach, and Abed-nego; these men, O king, have not regarded thee: they serve not thy gods, nor worship the golden image which thou hast set up. Then Nebuchadnezzar in his rage and fury commanded to bring Shadrach, Meshach, and Abed-nego. Then they brought these men before the king. Nebuchadnezzar spake and said unto them, Is it true, O Shadrach, Meshach, and Abed-nego, do not ye serve my gods, nor worship the golden image which I have set up? Now if ye be ready that at what time ye hear the sound of the cornet, flute, harp, sackbut, psaltery, and dulcimer, and all kinds of musick, ye fall down and worship the image which I have made; well: but if ye worship not, ye shall be cast the same hour into the midst of a burning fiery furnace; and who is that God that shall deliver you out of my hands?

—Daniel 3:1–15

## *The kingdom of darkness can be experienced by both the physical senses and the spiritual senses.*

The experience of the kingdom of darkness can be physical, and it can also be spiritual. I am sure every reader knows someone who has fallen into drug abuse, alcoholism, or despair. These are physical ills, but they also have the power to render the person under its influence spiritually bankrupt. Scripture warns us to stay away from the kingdom of darkness, its activities, values, principles, and standards.

Love not the world, neither the things that are in the world. If any man love the world, the love of the Father is not in him. For all that is in the world, the lust of the flesh, and the lust of the eyes, and the pride of life, is not of the Father, but is of the world. And the world passeth away, and the lust thereof: but he that doeth the will of God abideth for ever.

—1 John 2:15–17

Wherefore if ye be dead with Christ from the rudiments of the world, why, as though living in the world, are ye subject to ordinances, (Touch not; taste not; handle not…)

—COLOSSIANS 2:20–21

# The Kingdom of Darkness: An Elaborately Organized Kingdom

The kingdom of darkness is well-equipped and very ready to fight a pitched battle using any and all means at its disposal. Remember, you are engaged in a battle with a very organized system of protocol and change of command.

Finally, my brethren, be strong in the Lord, and in the power of his might. Put on the whole armour of God, that ye may be able to stand against the wiles of the devil. For we wrestle not against flesh and blood, but against principalities, against powers, against the rulers of the darkness of this world, against spiritual wickedness in high places.

—EPHESIANS 6:10–12

The following is a description of the kingdom of darkness. For some, this is the first time you are learning about the elaborately organized kingdom and nation of darkness. Like all good generals, it is to our benefit to be well aware of the tools at the enemy's disposal.

## 1. *Principalities*

The word *principality* comes from the Greek word *Archomai* which literally translated means "first in rank and order." Principalities derive their power directly from Satan and are the highest-ranking entities in Satan's army. They influence the affairs of humanity at a national level, impacting laws and policies. They are so purpose-specific that they often embody world leaders. Take Hitler, for instance. A careful examination of his life will undoubtedly point toward definite, demonic influence.

> To the intent that now unto the principalities and powers in heavenly places might be known by the church the manifold wisdom of God.
>
> —Ephesians 3:10

And the people with one accord gave heed unto those things which Philip spake, hearing and seeing the miracles which he did. For unclean spirits, crying with loud voice, came out of many that were possessed with them: and many taken with palsies, and that were lame, were healed. And there was great joy in that city. But there was a certain man, called Simon, which beforetime in the same city used sorcery, and bewitched the people of Samaria, giving out that himself was some great one: To whom they all gave heed, from the least to the greatest, saying, This man is the great power of God. And to him they had regard, because that of long time he had bewitched them with sorceries. But when they believed Philip preaching the things concerning the kingdom of God, and the name of Jesus Christ, they were baptized, both men and women. Then Simon himself believed also: and when he was baptized, he continued with Philip, and wondered, beholding the miracles and signs which were done. Now when the apostles which were at Jerusalem heard that Samaria had received the word of God, they sent unto them Peter and John: Who, when they were come down, prayed for them, that they might receive the Holy Ghost: (For as yet he was fallen upon none of them: only they were baptized in the name of the Lord Jesus.) Then laid they their hands on them, and they received the Holy Ghost. And when Simon saw that through laying on of the apostles' hands the Holy Ghost was given, he offered them money, Saying, Give me also this power, that on whomsoever I lay hands, he may receive the Holy Ghost. But Peter said unto him, Thy money perish with thee, because thou hast thought that the gift of God may be purchased with money. Thou hast neither part nor lot in this matter: for thy heart is not right in the sight of God. Repent therefore of this thy wickedness, and pray God, if perhaps the thought of thine heart may be forgiven thee. For I perceive that thou art in the gall of bitterness, and in the bond of iniquity. Then answered Simon, and said, Pray ye to the Lord for me, that none of these things which ye have spoken come upon me. And they, when they had testified and preached the word of the Lord, returned to Jerusalem, and preached the gospel in many villages of the Samaritans.

—ACTS 8:6–25

Moreover the word of the LORD came unto me, saying, Son of man, take up a lamentation upon the king of Tyrus, and say unto him, Thus saith the Lord GOD; Thou sealest up the sum, full of wisdom, and perfect in beauty. Thou hast been in Eden the garden of God; every precious stone was thy covering, the sardius, topaz, and the diamond, the beryl, the onyx, and the jasper, the sapphire, the emerald, and the carbuncle, and gold: the workmanship of thy tabrets and of thy pipes was prepared in thee in the day that thou wast created. Thou art the anointed cherub that covereth; and I have set thee so: thou wast upon the holy mountain of God; thou hast walked up and down in the midst of the stones of fire. Thou wast perfect in thy ways from the day that thou wast created, till iniquity was found in thee. By the multitude of thy merchandise they have filled the midst of thee with violence, and thou hast sinned: therefore I will cast thee as profane out of the mountain of God: and I will destroy thee, O covering cherub, from the midst of the stones of fire. Thine heart was lifted up because of thy beauty, thou hast corrupted thy wisdom by reason of thy brightness: I will cast thee to the ground, I will lay thee before kings, that they may behold thee. Thou hast defiled thy sanctuaries by the multitude of thine iniquities, by the iniquity of thy traffick; therefore will I bring forth a fire from the midst of thee, it shall devour thee, and I will bring thee to ashes upon the earth in the sight of all them that behold thee. All they that know thee among the people shall be astonished at thee: thou shalt be a terror, and never shalt thou be any more.

—Ezekiel 28:11–19

## 2. Powers

Next in the chain of command we find powers. The Greek word for power, *exousia*, speaks of delegated authority. These are demonic spirits that derive their jurisdictional and delegated authority from principalities. They affect and infect structures, systems, and the five pillars of our society: marriage, family, government, education, and church.

And having spoiled principalities and powers, he made a shew of them openly, triumphing over them in it.

—COLOSSIANS 2:15

The word of the LORD came again unto me, saying, Son of man, say unto the prince of Tyrus, Thus saith the Lord GOD; Because thine heart is lifted up, and thou hast said, I am a God, I sit in the seat of God, in the midst of the seas; yet thou art a man, and not God, though thou set thine heart as the heart of God: Behold, thou art wiser than Daniel; there is no secret that they can hide from thee: With thy wisdom and with thine understanding thou hast gotten thee riches, and hast gotten gold and silver into thy treasures: By thy great wisdom and by thy traffick hast thou increased thy riches, and thine heart is lifted up because of thy riches: Therefore thus saith the Lord GOD; Because thou hast set thine heart as the heart of God; Behold, therefore I will bring strangers upon thee, the terrible of the nations: and they shall draw their swords against the beauty of thy wisdom, and they shall defile thy brightness. They shall bring thee down to the pit, and thou shalt die the deaths of them that are slain in the midst of the seas. Wilt thou yet say before him that slayeth thee, I am God? but thou shalt be a man, and no God, in the hand of him that slayeth thee. Thou shalt die the deaths of the uncircumcised by the hand of strangers: for I have spoken it, saith the Lord GOD.

—EZEKIEL 28:1–10

### 3. Rulers of the darkness of this world

*Kosmokrator Skotosis* are the Greek words used for this category of spirits. These are spirits are very high-ranking officers that have specialized jurisdictional authority over the twelve cosmological systems of the universe and rule in the kingdom of darkness. They are responsible for literally blinding the minds of people to truth, and for facilitating sin, wickedness, and iniquity within the nations of this world. They are also responsible for keeping people in a state of darkness. (When I speak of darkness, I am not merely speaking of the absence of light, but the absence God. God is light and divine inspiration.) They affect the thoughts, feelings, and perceptions of humanity through mass media, music, movies, fashion, sports, philosophies, and religious ideologies.

> Who hath delivered us from the power of darkness, and hath translated us into the kingdom of his dear Son.
>
> —COLOSSIANS 1:13

> And the fifth angel poured out his vial upon the seat of the beast; and his kingdom was full of darkness; and they gnawed their tongues for pain.
>
> —REVELATION 16:10

> And the angels which kept not their first estate, but left their own habitation, he hath reserved in everlasting chains under darkness unto the judgment of the great day.
>
> —JUDE 1:6

> Raging waves of the sea, foaming out their own shame; wandering stars, to whom is reserved the

blackness of darkness for ever.

—Jude 1:13

## 4. *Spiritual wickedness in high places*

The Greek phrase, *Pneumatikos poneria epouranios,* speaks of types of spirits found in high and lofty places which are responsible for anything that is perverted, depraved, debased, warped, or corrupt. This spirit is spoken of as working from high, lofty, and heavenly places that not only speak of celestial zones and dimensions, but also the mind, which is a type of a heavenly place. It influences, seduces, and falsely inspires actions, perceptions, motivations, fantasies, imaginations, and appetites through the overt or covert attack and influence of the mind, affecting terrestrial and celestial domains. (See Jeremiah 1:10; Luke 11:16–26; Romans 8:14–23.) According to Daniel 10:10–13 these spirits operating in the second heaven frustrate and prohibit the manifestation and answers to believers' prayers. Perceptions, mindsets, paradigms, ideologies, and belief systems are twisted and perverted to accommodate the personality of these evil spirits.

> (For the weapons of our warfare are not carnal, but mighty through God to the pulling down of strong holds;) Casting down imaginations, and every high thing that exalteth itself against the knowledge of God, and bringing into captivity every thought to the obedience of Christ.
>
> —2 Corinthians 10:4–5

> And hath raised us up together, and made us sit together in heavenly places in Christ Jesus.
>
> —Ephesians 2:6

To the intent that now unto the principalities and powers in heavenly places might be known by the church the manifold wisdom of God.

—EPHESIANS 3:10

How art thou fallen from heaven, O Lucifer, son of the morning! how art thou cut down to the ground, which didst weaken the nations! For thou hast said in thine heart, I will ascend into heaven, I will exalt my throne above the stars of God: I will sit also upon the mount of the congregation, in the sides of the north: I will ascend above the heights of the clouds; I will be like the most High.

—ISAIAH 14:12–14

## 5. Devils and demons

Literally translated, the Greek term *daimon* means to distribute fortunes. A demon or devil is a supernatural spirit that possesses the nature of Satan and has the ability to give and distribute fortunes (mammon of the unrighteous), possess man, and control mindsets and activities. Devils can be worshiped, make people sick, communicate, and involve themselves in a host of other diabolical activities.

When the even was come, they brought unto him many that were possessed with devils: and he cast out the spirits with his word, and healed all that were sick.

—MATTHEW 8:16

And when he was come to the other side into the country of the Gergesenes, there met him two possessed with devils, coming out of the tombs, exceeding fierce, so that no man might pass by that way.

—MATTHEW 8:28

And I saw three unclean spirits like frogs come out of the mouth of the dragon, and out of the mouth of the beast, and out of the mouth of the false prophet. For they are the spirits of devils, working miracles, which go forth unto the kings of the earth and of the whole world, to gather them to the battle of that great day of God Almighty.

—REVELATION 16:13–14

No man can serve two masters: for either he will hate the one, and love the other; or else he will hold to the one, and despise the other. Ye cannot serve God and mammon.

—MATTHEW 6:24

### 6. *Spirits of the underworld*

These spirits work with high witchcraft operations. The underworld has six regions; none of which are places you would ever want to go:

- Death (1 Cor. 15:55; Job 34:22)
- Hell/Sheol/Hades (Isa. 14:19)
- The grave (Ezek. 31:15; Isa. 38:10)
- The pit (Ezek. 32:23)
- The abyss—the lower region of the pit (Isa. 38:17; Ps. 30:3)
- Regions of the sea (Ezek. 26:16; Job 41:1–31)

Hell from beneath is moved for thee to meet thee at thy coming: it stirreth up the dead for thee, even all the chief ones of the earth; it hath raised up from their thrones all the kings of the nations.

—ISAIAH 14:9

It came to pass also in the twelfth year, in the fifteenth day of the month, that the word of the LORD came unto me, saying, Son of man, wail for the multitude of Egypt, and cast them down, even her, and the daughters of the famous nations, unto the nether parts of the earth, with them that go down into the pit. Whom dost thou pass in beauty? go down, and be thou laid with the uncircumcised. They shall fall in the midst of them that are slain by the sword: she is delivered to the sword: draw her and all her multitudes. The strong among the mighty shall speak to him out of the midst of hell with them that help him: they are gone down, they lie uncircumcised, slain by the sword. Asshur is there and all her company: his graves are about him: all of them slain, fallen by the sword: Whose graves are set in the sides of the pit, and her company is round about her grave: all of them slain, fallen by the sword, which caused terror in the land of the living. There is Elam and all her multitude round about her grave, all of them slain, fallen by the sword, which are gone down uncircumcised into the nether parts of the earth, which caused their terror in the land of the living; yet have they borne their shame with them that go down to the pit. They have set her a bed in the midst of the slain with all her multitude: her graves are round about him: all of them uncircumcised, slain by the sword: though their terror was caused in the land of the living, yet have they borne their shame with them that go down to the pit: he is put in the midst of them that be slain. There is Meshech, Tubal, and all her multitude: her graves are round about him: all of them uncircumcised, slain by the sword, though they caused their terror in the land of the living. And they shall not lie with the mighty that are fallen of the uncircumcised, which are gone down to hell with their weapons of war: and they have laid their swords under their heads, but their iniquities shall be upon their bones, though they were the terror of the mighty in the land of the living. Yea, thou shalt be broken in the midst of the uncircumcised, and shalt lie with them that are slain with the sword. There is Edom, her kings, and all her princes, which with their might are laid by them that were slain by the sword: they shall lie with the uncircumcised, and with them that go down to the pit. There be the princes of the north, all of them, and all the Zidonians, which are gone down with the slain; with their terror they are ashamed of their might; and they lie uncircumcised with them that be slain by the sword, and bear their shame with them that go down to the pit. Pharaoh shall see them, and shall be comforted over all his multitude, even Pharaoh and all his army slain by the sword, saith the Lord GOD. For I have caused my terror in the land of the living: and he shall be laid in the midst of the uncircumcised with them that are slain with the sword, even Pharaoh and all his multitude, saith the Lord GOD.

—EZEKIEL 32:17–32

Canst thou draw out leviathan with an hook? or his tongue with a cord which thou lettest down? Canst thou put an hook into his nose? or bore his jaw through with a thorn? Will he make many supplications unto thee? will he speak soft words unto thee? Will he make a covenant with thee? wilt thou take him for a servant for ever? Wilt thou play with him as with a bird? or wilt thou bind him for thy maidens? Shall the companions make a banquet of him? shall they part him among the merchants? Canst thou fill his skin with barbed iron? or his head with fish spears? Lay thine hand upon him, remember the battle, do no more. Behold, the hope of him is in vain: shall not one be cast down even at the sight of him? None is so fierce that dare stir him up: who then is able to stand before me? Who hath prevented me, that I should repay him? whatsoever is under the whole heaven is mine. I will not conceal his parts, nor his power, nor his comely proportion. Who can discover the face of his garment? or who can come to him with his double bridle? Who can open the doors of his face? his teeth are terrible round about. His scales are his pride, shut up together as with a close seal. One is so near to another, that no air can come between them. They are joined one to another, they stick together, that they cannot be sundered. By his neesings a light doth shine, and his eyes are like the eyelids of the morning. Out of his mouth go burning lamps, and sparks of fire leap out. Out of his nostrils goeth smoke, as out of a seething pot or caldron. His breath kindleth coals, and a flame goeth out of his mouth. In his neck remaineth strength, and sorrow is turned into joy before him. The flakes of his flesh are joined together: they are firm in themselves; they cannot be moved. His heart is as firm as a stone; yea, as hard as a piece of the nether millstone. When he raiseth up himself, the mighty are afraid: by reason of breakings they purify themselves. The sword of him that layeth at him cannot hold: the spear, the dart, nor the habergeon. He esteemeth iron as straw, and brass as rotten wood. The arrow cannot make him flee: slingstones are turned with him into stubble. Darts are counted as stubble: he laugheth at the shaking of a spear. Sharp stones are under him: he spreadeth sharp pointed things upon the mire. He maketh the deep to boil like a pot: he maketh the sea like a pot of ointment. He maketh a path to shine after him; one would think the deep to be hoary. Upon earth there is not his like, who is made without fear. He beholdeth all high things: he is a king over all the children of pride.

—JOB 41:1–34

## 7. Spirit birds

Remember when Noah sent out the dove, who returned with an olive branch, or when God used a bird to bring food to Elijah the prophet? Satan also has spirit birds at his disposal, only they are unclean and hateful.

And he cried mightily with a strong voice, saying, Babylon the great is fallen, is fallen, and is become the habitation of devils, and the hold of every foul spirit, and a cage of every unclean and hateful bird.

—REVELATION 18:2

## 8. Spirit horses and horsemen

Before there were tanks, airplanes, and Scud missiles, men used horses and horsemen when they went to war. As in the natural, so it is in the spiritual. The spiritual battlefield is filled with spirit horses and horsemen.

And the four angels were loosed, which were prepared for an hour, and a day, and a month, and a
year, for to slay the third part of men. And the number of the army of the horsemen were two hundred
thousand thousand: and I heard the number of them.
And thus I saw the horses in the vision, and them
that sat on them, having breastplates of fire, and of
jacinth, and brimstone: and the heads of the horses
were as the heads of lions; and out of their mouths
issued fire and smoke and brimstone. By these three
was the third part of men killed, by the fire, and by
the smoke, and by the brimstone, which issued out of
their mouths. For their power is in their mouth, and
in their tails: for their tails were like unto serpents,
and had heads, and with them they do hurt.

—Revelation 9:15–19

Speak to Zerubbabel, governor of Judah, saying,
I will shake the heavens and the earth; and I will
overthrow the throne of kingdoms, And I will
destroy the strength of the kingdoms of the heathen; and I will overthrow the chariots, and those
that ride in them; and the horses and their riders
shall come down, every one by the sword of his
brother.

—Haggai 2:21–22

### 9. Familiar spirits

We can encounter familiar spirits who work for Satan.
They are like reconnaissance teams. Their job is to spy
and take reports back to headquarters.

And the soul that turneth after such as have familiar spirits, and after wizards, to go a whoring after them, I will even set my face against that soul, and will cut him off from among his people.

—Leviticus 20:6

### 10. Unclean spirits

Satan even commands unclean spirits—yes, the same spirits Jesus cast out. As the Word suggests, this spirit is responsible for lewd, promiscuous, and immoral activities.

And they were all amazed, insomuch that they questioned among themselves, saying, What thing is this? what new doctrine is this? for with authority commandeth he even the unclean spirits, and they do obey him.

—Mark 1:27

### 11. Evil spirits

Satan commands vicious and malicious spirits that are responsible for promoting terrible, dehumanized conditions. They work in concert with other spirits to cause misfortunes, mishaps, accidents, and incite criminal activities.

And in that same hour he cured many of their infirmities and plagues, and of evil spirits; and unto many that were blind he gave sight.

—Luke 7:21

### 12. Seducing spirits

Satan commands seducing spirits, which are responsible for attracting and drawing you into a wrong or foolish course of action. Many fall victim to this kind of spirit.

Now the Spirit speaketh expressly, that in the latter

times some shall depart from the faith, giving heed to seducing spirits, and doctrines of devils.

—1 TIMOTHY 4:1

## 13. Archangels

Satan was a created being, along with all other angelic beings. He was also one of the highest-ranking angels, along with Michael and Gabriel. According to Jeremiah 4:23–26, Ezekiel 28:11–17, and other passages of Scripture, Satan had a kingdom on earth. He fell and led a host of angels into rebellion against God. He was thrown out of heaven, and has become a ruler of this world's systems: the prince of the power of the air. He is cunning, wicked, and insidious. He opposes all that is of God and everything that is good.

How art thou fallen from heaven, O Lucifer, son of the morning! how art thou cut down to the ground, which didst weaken the nations! For thou hast said in thine heart, I will ascend into heaven, I will exalt my throne above the stars of God: I will sit also upon the mount of the congregation, in the sides of the north: I will ascend above the heights of the clouds; I will be like the most High.

—ISAIAH 14:12–14

With the work of an engraver in stone, like the engravings of a signet, shalt thou engrave the two stones with the names of the children of Israel: thou shalt make them to be set in ouches of gold. And thou shalt put the two stones upon the shoulders of the ephod for stones of memorial unto the children of Israel: and Aaron shall bear their names before the LORD upon his two shoulders for a memorial. And thou shalt make ouches of gold; And two chains of pure gold at the ends; of wreathen work shalt thou make them, and fasten the wreathen chains to the ouches. And thou shalt make the breastplate of judgment with cunning work; after the work of the ephod thou shalt make it; of gold, of blue, and of purple, and of scarlet, and of fine twined linen, shalt thou make it. Four-square it shall be being doubled; a span shall be the length thereof, and a span shall be the breadth thereof. And thou shalt set in it settings of stones, even four rows of stones: the first row shall be a sardius, a topaz, and a carbuncle: this shall be the first row.

—EXODUS 28:11–17

Most of us know that Satan has more than one name. On our battlefield it is better for us to be prepared by knowing these names:

1. Lucifer (Isa. 14:12–14)
2. Devil and Satan (Rev. 12:9)
3. Beelzebub (Matt. 10:25; 12:24)
4. Adversary (1 Pet. 5:8–9)
5. Belial (2 Cor. 6:15)
6. Dragon (Rev. 12:3–12; 13:1–4; 20:1–3)
7. Serpent (2 Cor. 11:3; Rev. 12:9)
8. The god of this world (2 Cor. 4:4)
9. The prince of this world (John 12:31)
10. Prince of the power of the air (Eph. 2:1–3)
11. Accuser of the Brethren (Rev. 12:10)
12. The enemy (Matt. 13:39)

13. Tempter (Matt. 4:3)
14. The wicked one (Matt. 13:19, 38)

## The Nature of Satanic Spirits

Readers need to know the nature of satanic beings. People often make the error of believing Satan as a caricatured being with red horns and a pitchfork. Satan is much more than that—and he is powerful:

1. They are not human (Mark 10:8)
2. They are evil (Judges 9:23)
3. They are intelligent and wise (1 Kings 22:22–24)
4. They are powerful (Mark 5:1–18)
5. They are beings with personalities (Mark 11:6–9)
6. They talk and communicate (Mark 5:6–7)
7. They feel (Mark 8:29)
8. They have knowledge (Acts 19:15)
9. They congregate and fellowship (1 Cor. 10:20–21)
10. They "preach" doctrines (1 Tim. 4:1)
11. They have desires (Matt. 8:28–31)
12. They have a will (Matt. 12:43–45)
13. They can work miracles (Rev. 16:13–14)
14. They possess supernatural strength (Mark 5:1–18)
15. They fear God (James 2:19)
16. They travel (Mark 5:7, 12)
17. They impersonate people (1 Sam. 28:3–9)
18. They know their fate (Matt. 8:31–32)

19. They recognize those who have power over them (Acts 19:13–15)
20. They are responsible for every evil known to man (Luke 7:21)

## The Scope of Their Activities and Proof of Their Presence

The scope of demonic activities is both broad and diverse. Among them are:

1. Deafness (Matt. 9:32–33)
2. Blindness (Matt. 12:22)
3. Grief (1 Sam. 1:7–8)
4. Vexation (Matt. 15:22)
5. Provocation (1 Chron. 21:1)
6. Murder (Ps. 106:36, 38)
7. Suicide (Matt. 17:15)
8. Idolatry (1 Kings 22:53)
9. Convulsions (Mark 9:20)
10. Lusts (John 8:44)
11. Confusion and strife (James 3:15–16)
12. False worship (Deut. 32:17)
13. Error, heresy, and false doctrine (1 Tim. 4:1–2)
14. Sickness and disease (Matt. 4:23–24)
15. Torments (Matt. 15:22)
16. Deception (1 John 4:1–6)
17. Lying (1 Kings 22:21–24)
18. Wickedness (Luke 11:26)
19. Fear (2 Tim. 1:7)
20. Worldliness (1 John 2:15–17)
21. Bondage (Rom. 8:15)
22. Discord (1 Kings 22:21–24)

23. Violence (Mark 9:22)
24. Betrayal (John 13:2)
25. Oppression (Acts 10:38)
26. Persecution (Rev. 2:10)
27. Jealousy (1 Sam. 19:1–11)
28. False Prophecy (1 Sam. 18:8–10)
29. Stealing (John 10:10)
30. Fighting/wrestling (Eph. 6:10–18)

# Strategies and Tactics for Spiritual Warfare

BINDING THE STRONGMAN is a biblical discipline taught by Jesus Christ. It is a tool Christians can use to fight against the powers of the dark kingdom. Let us examine the use of this tool in Scripture:

And he was casting out a devil, and it was dumb. And it came to pass, when the devil was gone out, the dumb spake; and the people wondered. But some of them said, He casteth out devils through Beelzebub the chief of the devils. And others, tempting him, sought of him a sign from heaven. But he, knowing their thoughts, said unto them, Every kingdom divided against itself is brought to desolation; and a house divided against a house falleth. If Satan also be divided against himself, how shall his kingdom stand? because ye say that I cast out devils through Beelzebub. And if I by Beelzebub cast out devils, by whom do your sons cast them out? therefore shall they be your judges. But if I with the finger of God cast out devils, no doubt the kingdom of God is come upon you. When a strong man armed keepeth his palace, his goods are in peace: but when a stronger than he shall come upon him, and overcome him, he taketh from him all his armour wherein he trusted, and divideth his spoils. He that is not with me is against me: and he that gathereth not with me scattereth. When the unclean spirit is gone out of a man, he walketh through dry places, seeking rest; and finding none, he saith, I will return unto my house whence I came out. And when he cometh, he findeth it swept and garnished. Then goeth he, and taketh to him seven other spirits more wicked than himself; and they enter in, and dwell there: and the last state of that man is worse than the first.

—LUKE 11:14–26

*When you engage in the administration of deliverance, you must ensure you are biblically correct.*

Use this book with confidence knowing that, according to 1 John 3:8, this was the purpose for which "the Son of God was manifested, that he might destroy the works of the devil." May the Spirit of the Lord rest upon you so that all your endeavors are initiated by and subject to the Spirit of the Lord.

The Spirit of the Lord is upon me, because he hath anointed me to preach the gospel to the poor; he hath sent me to heal the brokenhearted, to preach deliverance to the captives, and recovering of sight to the blind, to set at liberty them that are bruised.

—LUKE 4:18

*As you pray you must totally rely on the Holy Spirit.*
Even as the Holy Spirit led Jesus in all things, He must also lead you. Do not be presumptuous when it comes to determining who needs deliverance and who does not. The Holy Spirit operates like the sonar equipment deep-sea divers use to fathom the depths of the ocean. The Holy Spirit is He who has the ability to search and fathom the hearts of men. First Corinthians 2:10 states, "But God hath revealed them unto us by his Spirit: for the Spirit searcheth all things, yea, the deep things of God." He will help you to discern, test, resist, and reject demonic spirits and their activities.

To another the working of miracles; to another prophecy; to another discerning of spirits; to another divers kinds of tongues; to another the interpretation of tongues.

—1 CORINTHIANS 12:10

Be sober, be vigilant; because your adversary the devil, as a roaring lion, walketh about, seeking whom he may devour: Whom resist stedfast in the faith, knowing that the same afflictions are accomplished in your brethren that are in the world.

—1 PETER 5:8–9

Beloved, believe not every spirit, but try the spirits whether they are of God: because many false prophets are gone out into the world. Hereby know ye the Spirit of God: Every spirit that confesseth that Jesus Christ is come in the flesh is of God: and every spirit that confesseth not that Jesus Christ is come in the flesh is not of God: and this is that spirit of antichrist, whereof ye have heard that it should come; and even now already is it in the world. Ye are of God, little children, and have overcome them: because greater is he that is in you, than he that is in the world. They are of the world: therefore speak they of the world, and the world heareth them. We are of God: he that knoweth God heareth us; he that is not of God heareth not us. Hereby know we the spirit of truth, and the spirit of error.

—1 JOHN 4:1–6

Likewise the Spirit also helpeth our infirmities: for we know not what we should pray for as we ought: but the Spirit itself maketh intercession for us with groanings which cannot be uttered.

—ROMANS 8:26

Since the Holy Spirit knows the hearts of men, He can communicate His knowledge to you as a believer during your prayer and intercession. You then will be empowered by God to act in accordance with the promptings, stirrings, leading, and insight the Holy Spirit gives. Remember, one of your greatest defense mechanisms is to stay connected with the Holy Spirit as you pray.

### *Charge yourself up in the Holy Spirit.*
Just as a car battery can run out of power, or a cell phone runs out of power, necessitating a recharge, the believer can recharge his spiritual battery by praying in

the Holy Spirit. This discipline should be a part of your daily prayer vigil. It is also a wonderful means by which spiritual power is accrued for prayer and during prayer.

He that speaketh in an unknown tongue edifieth himself.

—1 CORINTHIANS 14:4

But ye, beloved, building up yourselves on your most holy faith, praying in the Holy Ghost.

—JUDE 20

### *Take dominion.*

Use authority in the name of Jesus, and don't be afraid to take dominion over the strongman. Matthew 16:19 states that God has given us "the keys of the kingdom of heaven: and whatsoever thou shalt bind on earth shall be bound in heaven: and whatsoever thou shalt loose on earth shall be loosed in heaven."

One of your kingdom keys that will enhance your prayer life is the discipline of "binding and loosing." Matthew 18:18 states, "Verily I say unto you, whatsoever ye shall bind on earth shall be bound in heaven: and whatsoever ye shall loose on earth shall be loosed in heaven."

This is like drawing up contracts that must be adhered to in the realm of the spirit. As it relates to demonic forces and activities, binding immobilizes demonic activities by imposing or commanding adherence to a specific alternative directive. Loosing is the opposite of binding. It extricates, discharges, and releases demonic forces from specific directive or obligatory activity. Since Matthew 18:18 seems to indicate that binding and loosing are inextricably connected, then we must consider binding and loosing as a single key. If you are going to bind, you must loose; if you are going to loose, you must bind. You cannot use one without the other. The question I'm most frequently asked is, "What do I bind, and what do I loose?" Simply put, you bind the activities of Satan and his cohorts; you loose any effect that their presence has had, and then you release the kingdom (God's divine rule) counterpart. The devil has no choice in the matter. When it comes to spiritual warfare, do not accept substitutes or compromises. Do not back off, back down, give up, or give in. God has given you authority over all of the devil's ability according to Luke 10:19. Ephesians 1:20–23 states that Satan is under your feet. That means that he does not have authority over you, but you have authority over him. Binding and loosing is a way to control satanic activities. Scripture clearly states that every believer has been given authority over the works of the enemy. You must rise up and take the authority by superimposing the will of God over the will and all activity of the enemy. He is operating illegally in the earth realm. May I remind you that he is not the prince of the power of the earth, but *the prince of the power of the air* according to Ephesians 2:2. Therefore, rise up and take your rightful position as God's deputized agent. Insist that he complies with the biblically-based terms issued by you. The Bible states that in your kingly posture, you have been given power to decree a thing, and it will be established. (See Job 22:28.) When you decree a thing in Jesus' name, the enemy is aware that you are not suggesting or even giving him an option or advice. He understands that when you come in Jesus' name he must cease and desist his illegal activities at once! Why? Because in Isaiah 45:23, God Himself states, "I have sworn by myself, the word is gone out of my mouth in righteousness, and shall not return, That unto me every knee shall bow, every tongue shall swear," and it is further stated in Philippians 2:10–11, "That at the name of Jesus every knee should bow, of things in heaven, and things in earth, and things under the earth; and that every tongue should confess that Jesus Christ is Lord, to the glory of God the Father."

### *Become proficient in the mechanics of binding and loosing.*

When we are born we do not know how to do anything. Over time, we learn to roll over, sit up, crawl, walk, and run. Even if you have no experience in binding or loosing prayer and work, you can become proficient at it through practice, study, and training. Remember, you have to start crawling before you walk and run.

> Or else how can one enter into a strong man's house, and spoil his goods, except he first bind the strong man? and then he will spoil his house.
>
> —MATTHEW 12:29

> Verily I say unto you, Whatsoever ye shall bind on earth shall be bound in heaven: and whatsoever ye shall loose on earth shall be loosed in heaven.
>
> —MATTHEW 18:18

Binding can be likened to a person issuing a restraining order from the court of heaven on behalf of God, who sits as the judge of the earth. A restraining order is a legal document and the recipient must comply with the terms outlined therein. Likewise, whatever you decree and declare, the enemy, along with his cohorts, must comply. They are bound by the blood, the Word, and the Spirit.

To loose is the opposite of bind. Demonic spirits have received orders from Satan and other demonic personalities existing in the higher echelon of the satanic kingdom. When you loose, you superimpose a new set of orders that are also binding by the blood, the Word, and the Spirit. When employing this strategy you are not only loosing a spirit, but you are also loosing the effects that spirit had on a person, place, or thing.

**Bind:** The principality and the subordinate spirits in the name of Jesus, and make them part of the footstool of Jesus, according to Luke 20:43 and Acts 2:35.

**Loose:** The effects of their assignment. When Jesus administered deliverance to people there was evidence that not only was the strongman and spirit gone, the effects of their presence were gone as well.

> And, behold, there was a woman which had a spirit of infirmity eighteen years, and was bowed together, and could in no wise lift up herself. And when Jesus saw her, he called her to him, and said unto her, Woman, thou art loosed from thine infirmity. And he laid his hands on her: and immediately she was made straight, and glorified God.
>
> —LUKE 13:11–13

Release: The kingdom alternative. Mark 5:15 states: "And they come to Jesus, and see him that was possessed with the devil, and had the legion, sitting, and clothed, and in his right mind: and they were afraid."

The following are simple principles to follow:

- Establish your legal rights and authority in Christ Jesus.

- Use the name of Jesus (never assume you have power in and of yourself).

- Determine the strongman and subordinate spirits.

- Bind their works, and make them a part of the footstool of Jesus.

- Remind demonic spirits that they must comply because Jesus came to "destroy the works of the devil" (1 John 3:8).

- Loose every sign, symptom, and condition associated with their presence.

- Release the kingdom of heaven counterpart.

- Reinforce your prayer life with fasting.

- Remain submitted to the Spirit of the Lord.

- Resist the devil, and he will flee.

- Use the Word of the Lord.

### *Do not allow any strongholds to remain.*

- Declare and decree that all materials used to construct the strongholds are now demolished and utterly destroyed.

- Ask the Holy Spirit to demolish strongholds and to sweep all residue away.

### *Close doors and establish God as the new Doorkeeper and Gatekeeper of:*

- The city

- The country
- The nation

The Bible declares that the power of our words affect change in our lives, homes, environment, communities, cities, and nations. Pray for the peace of the city so that you can have peace as well.

> Lift up your head, O ye gates; and be ye lift up, ye everlasting doors; and the King of glory shall come in. Who is this King of glory? The LORD strong and mighty, the LORD mighty in battle. Lift up your heads, O ye gates; even lift them up, ye everlasting doors; and the King of glory shall come in. Who is this King of glory? The LORD of hosts, he is the King of glory. Selah.
>
> —PSALM 24:7–10

> Except the LORD build the house, they labour in vain that build it: except the LORD keep the city, the watchman waketh but in vain.
>
> —PSALM 127:1

- Your personage, family, or ministry

> Yet a man is risen to pursue thee, and to seek thy soul: but the soul of my lord shall be bound in the bundle of life with the LORD thy God; and the souls of thine enemies, them shall he sling out, as out of the middle of a sling.
>
> —1 SAMUEL 25:29

> He will not suffer thy foot to be moved: he that keepeth thee will not slumber. Behold, he that keepeth

Israel shall neither slumber nor sleep.

—Psalm 121:3–4

### *Establish your legal right in the name of Jesus.*

Using the name of Jesus means that your activities are backed up in the power and authority of the Anointed One of God, who declared the extent, power, and magnitude of His anointing in the following verse:

> And Jesus came and spake unto them, saying, All power is given unto me in heaven and in earth. Go ye therefore, and teach all nations, baptizing them in the name of the Father, and of the Son, and of the Holy Ghost: Teaching them to observe all things whatsoever I have commanded you: and, lo, I am with you alway, even unto the end of the world. Amen.
>
> —Matthew 28:18–20

### *Identify the strongman and the subordinate spirits.*

Using this manual is simple. You can go to the table of contents and identify the strongman, then go to the corresponding page for details of subordinate spirits, their signs, symptoms, and manifestations. Or you can use the index in the back of the book to identify the spirit or strongman alphabetized for ease of reference. Regarding the strongman, you will find that there are several subordinate spirits that operate with each. My suggestion is to explore each strongman that relate to a specific spirit. Ask God how to proceed in prayer. He might instruct you to war against one or all of them.

### *Utilize the prayer journal.*

See the front cover for ordering information. This prayer journal will make your prayer time more effective.

# Spirit of Absalom

ABSALOM IS A renegade spirit who uses seduction and pretense in order to fulfill his diabolical operations. His activities are designed to undermine and destroy purpose, potential, and the influence and authority of men and women of God who hold strategic positions in the kingdom of God. He forms a very strong alliance with the spirit of Ahithophel in order to execute his strategies and plans. Together they form a very strong confederation. Second Samuel 15:12 states "Absalom sent for Ahithophel the Gilonite, David's counsellor, from his city, even from Giloh, while he offered sacrifices. And the conspiracy was strong; for the people increased continually with Absalom." He identifies himself with people who harbor bitterness and unforgiveness, who under normal circumstances would allow these spirits to fester without acting upon them. Once these individuals connect they begin to move with a vengeance, forcefully and decisively sticking at the nerve center of an organization, ministry, or relationship until it is brought under their control and authority. Read 2 Samuel 13:1 through 19:8 for greater understanding.

> And one told David, saying, Ahithophel is among the conspirators with Absalom. And David said, O LORD, I pray thee, turn the counsel of Ahithophel into foolishness.
>
> —2 SAMUEL 15:31

It divides and conquers, transferring loyalty from one person to another. It also works well with the spirit of perversion. This spirit defies divine authority and attempts to deny a believer his basic human and kingdom rights.

## Signs, Symptoms, and Manifestations of the Spirit of Absalom

| | | |
|---|---|---|
| Defiance | Deception | Rebellion |
| Pride | Vanity | Lying |
| Perversion | Lust | Power struggle |
| Cunning craftiness | Seduction | Self-righteousness |
| Self-exaltation | Treachery | Hypocrisy |
| Conspiracy | Pretense | Divided allegiance |
| Usurping authority | Haughtiness | Irreverence |
| Diabolical alliance | Murder | Sedition |
| Treason | Hostility | Betrayal |

| Jealousy | Disrespect | Plotting the demise of power, influence, and respect |
|---|---|---|
| Undermining ministry and influence | | |

**Release:** The spirit of submission, integrity, purpose, timing of the Lord, the heart of a servant, integrity, humility, apostolic anointing, wisdom, peace, truth, and prophetic intercession.

# Spirit of Addiction

An addiction is a complex illness with physical and psychological symptoms and wide-scale social ramifications. It not only affects the person but also his family, friends, and social environment. Naturally speaking, the way to recovery is long and painful, and there is always the danger of relapsing. However, with God all things are possible. Popular conceptions of addiction have been expanded to include gambling, eating chocolate, playing computer games, and even using the Internet. These non-drug, addictive behaviors are similar to any drug addiction in that the person lacks control over his activities and behaviors. Instead the activities and behavior have taken control over the individual. The enemy is sophisticated in keeping people in bondage. As humanity progresses, he continues to reinvent himself and forge new weapons of mass destruction.

There are popular and professional definitions of what an addiction is. In everyday language, we think of someone who is addicted to something as having what we could call an unhealthy habit. But those of us who are mature in the Lord know that behind these so-called addictions are demonic spirits.

An addiction is an progressive abuse of something that is difficult or impossible to control. Some of the things listed below, however, may in some cases be more correctly termed compulsions or obsessions. There is still some debate about the differences but basically an addiction is something which you enjoy doing, or started off enjoying, and involves some degree of physical dependence. An obsession on the other hand is an idea or thought dominating a person's mind. A compulsion is an irresistible urge or repetitive behavior often performed in response to an obsession.

Addictions can be categorized by the following:

**Substance:** alcohol, heroin, tobacco, solvents, cocaine, cannabis, caffeine, methadone, benzodiazepines, hallucinogens, amphetamines, ecstasy, painkillers, barbiturates, and steroids.

**Social:** exercise, sex, sexual perversion, pornography, eating (anorexia, bulimia), techno (computer games, cybersex, Internet), work, gambling, oniomania (shopping).

| Signs, Symptoms, and Manifestations of Addiction | | |
|---|---|---|
| Alcoholism | Pedophilia | Voyeurism |
| Pornography | Cyber-sex | Adultery |
| Drug abuse | Oniomia | Idolatry |
| Compulsive spending | Denial | Lying |
| Greed | Filthy lucre | Compromise |

| Temptation | Iniquity | Sin |
|---|---|---|
| Bulimia | Anorexia | Over-eating |
| Dependency | Codependency | Victimization |
| Shame | Violence | Death |
| Dreams | Disillusion | Hallucination |
| Nightmares | Psychosis | Neurosis |
| Suicide | Depression | Afflictions |
| Deception | Selfishness | Self-centeredness |
| Stealing | Dysfunctions | Self-loathing |
| Contaminated anointing | Betrayal | Carnality |
| Eating disorders | Psychotic behavior | Perversion |
| Inordinate affections | Misrepresentation | Worldliness |
| Social/relational violations | Secretism | Masturbation |
| Lack of control | Compulsive activities | Habits |
| Snares | Riotous living | Deceit |
| Fear | Anxiety | Bondages |
| Uncleanness | Withdrawal | Defiance |
| Oppression | Vitiation of will | Slavery |
| Pride | Independent spirit | Stubborn |
| Terror | Manipulation | Destruction |
| Railing | Obstinance | Secularism |
| Spiritual darkness | Traditional entrenchment | Crookedness |
| Murder/abortion | Antichrist activities | Psychological bondage |

| Gross darkness | Crime | Abuse |
|---|---|---|
| Money laundering | Hatred | Role reversal |
| Prostitution | Antagonism | Lusts |
| Suspicion | Prostitution | Obsessions |
| Mental breakdowns | Kleptomania | Gambling |
| Seduction | Homosexuality | Sadomasochism |
| Masochism | Dishonesty | Dishonor |
| Emotional disturbance | Hypersensitivity | Obsessive-compulsive disorder |

**Release:** Salvation, healing balm of Gilead, purpose, timing of the Lord, the heart of a servant, integrity, apostolic anointing, peace, truth, fruit of the Spirit, fear of the Lord, discipline, and honesty.

# Spirit of Affinity

JUST AS ITS name suggests, this spirit loves its assignment. As you begin to study this spirit you will realize that it logically falls into five categories: soul ties, familiar spirits, spirits of inheritance/generational curses, carnality, and unholy alliances. Although each of the aforementioned play an integral role with this strongman, and form a very solid bond, we will deal with the strongman of carnality as a separate heading and soul ties, familiar spirits, and spirits of inheritance and unholy alliances under this heading.

## 1. Soul ties

This is a spirit that has the power to attract and unite. It creates a force of connectedness (covenants) between two entities or individuals for the purpose of the reinforcement of divine or diabolical intents. Concerning diabolical intents and purposes, the ultimate aim is to distract and derail an individual, thus destroying his chances of fulfilling purpose, maximizing his potential and reaching his destiny. This spirit robs entities of his innocence, purity, sincerity, and focus, and often acts as a doorkeeper for other spirits. First Kings 11:1–13 records how Solomon had soul ties with many women. This led to the downfall of his kingdom. At this junction, it is important that you understand the nature of soul ties. Not every soul tie is diabolical, such as marriage, friendship, and family soul ties. However, the enemy can use these God-given relationships, and twist and pervert them in order to fulfill his plans and purposes. Soul ties fall under the following two categories:

## Divine (Legitimate)

Marriage (1 Kings 11:1–10)
Friendships (1 Kings 12:6–21)
Family/In-laws (2 Samuel 13:1–22)
Ecclesiastical Relationships (Ephesians 4:16)
Covering/Mentorship/Leadership (2 Kings 18:1–5; 1
    Chronicles 11:1–25)

## Satanic

Relational (Numbers 33:55)
Sexual Partners (1 Corinthians 6:13–18)
Demonic (Mark 5:1–10)
Organizational (Luke 11:52–12:3)
Lodges and other secret organizations
Religious/Cultic organizations

Even as divine soul ties, such as marriages and friendships, are formed for a specific purpose, so are diabolical soul ties formed to accomplish a specific purpose. In the case of Solomon and his many wives, they brought with them satanically-provoked customs, habits, and religious practices, which presented an open door in Solomon's life, and the lives of those of over whom he had rule. The issue with diabolical soul ties is not just the fact of spiritual abortion occurring in your life, but also the potential of negatively affecting everyone within your sphere of influence. Solomon's capricious activities and love for many women created the perfect scenario for Satan to take an entire nation into bondage.

> But king Solomon loved many strange women, together with the daughter of Pharaoh, women of the Moabites, Ammonites, Edomites, Zidonians, and Hittites; Of the nations concerning which the LORD said unto the children of Israel, Ye shall not go in to them, neither shall they come in unto you: for surely they will turn away your heart after their gods: Solomon clave unto these in love. And he had seven hundred wives, princesses, and three hundred concubines: and his wives turned away his heart. For it came to pass, when Solomon was old, that his wives turned away his heart after other gods: and his heart was not perfect with the LORD his God, as was the heart of David his father. For Solomon went after Ashtoreth the goddess of the Zidonians, and after Milcom the abomination of the Ammonites. And Solomon did evil in the sight of the LORD, and went not fully after the LORD, as did David his father. Then did Solomon build an high place for Chemosh, the abomination of Moab, in the hill that is before Jerusalem, and for Molech, the abomination of the children of Ammon. And likewise did he

for all his strange wives, which burnt incense and sacrificed unto their gods. And the LORD was angry with Solomon, because his heart was turned from the LORD God of Israel, which had appeared unto him twice, And had commanded him concerning this thing, that he should not go after other gods: but he kept not that which the LORD commanded. Wherefore the LORD said unto Solomon, Forasmuch as this is done of thee, and thou hast not kept my covenant and my statutes, which I have commanded thee, I will surely rend the kingdom from thee, and will give it to thy servant. Notwithstanding in thy days I will not do it for David thy father's sake: but I will rend it out of the hand of thy son. Howbeit I will not rend away all the kingdom; but will give one tribe to thy son for David my servant's sake, and for Jerusalem's sake which I have chosen. And the LORD stirred up an adversary unto Solomon, Hadad the Edomite: he was of the king's seed in Edom. For it came to pass, when David was in Edom, and Joab the captain of the host was gone up to bury the slain, after he had smitten every male in Edom; (For six months did Joab remain there with all Israel, until he had cut off every male in Edom:) That Hadad fled, he and certain Edomites of his father's servants with him, to go into Egypt; Hadad being yet a little child. And they arose out of Midian, and came to Paran: and they took men with them out of Paran, and they came to Egypt, unto Pharaoh king of Egypt; which gave him an house, and appointed him victuals, and gave him land. And Hadad found great favour in the sight of Pharaoh, so that he gave him to wife the sister of his own wife, the sister of Tahpenes the queen. And the sister of Tahpenes bare him Genubath his son, whom Tahpenes weaned in Pharaoh's house: and Genubath was in Pharaoh's household among the sons of Pharaoh.

—1 KINGS 11:1–41

## 2. Familiar spirits

Familiar spirits are demonic agents whose main assignment is to become well acquainted with a person or groups of persons. The term *familiar* refers to a relational aspect of their association in that they identify themselves with a particular person or group of people. In the Old Testament we find that familiar spirits are mentioned in several places: Leviticus 19:31, 20:6, 20:27; Deuteronomy 18:9–14; 2 Kings 21:6, 23:24; 1 Chronicles 10:13–14; 2 Chronicles 33:6; Isaiah 8:19, to name a few. In the New Testament, we clearly see familiar spirits at work. A few examples can be found in Matthew 9:32, 12:43–45, 15:22, 17:15–18; Mark 5:1–20, 9:17–26; Acts 16:16–18, 19:15–16.

These demonic spirits propagate the will of their master, Satan. They are responsible for satanic surveillance, diabolical reconnaissance, and vigilante activities. They are spirits with assignments emanating from a highly developed and complex satanic operation designed to kill, steal, and destroy. In order for you to understand their functions, roles, and portfolio, modern computer terminologies will explain some of their activities. They gather information through observation, and create a comprehensive dossier on the person to whom they are assigned. This information would then be passed on to another recording spirit to be downloaded into satanic databases for future reference. If Paul was born during this century, perhaps "the handwriting" he refers to in Colossians 2:14 would read *database*.

Familiar spirits usually operate independently of the human spirit. However, they have also been known to possess human beings who become agents. In 1 Samuel 28:7 Saul sought a woman who operated by familiar spirits. He told his servants to "Seek me a woman that hath a familiar spirit, that I may go to her, and enquire of her. And his servants said to him, Behold, there is a woman that hath a familiar spirit at Endor."

In this text a familiar spirit has formed an unholy alliance with the witch of Endor who crosses over to the "dark" world and sees demonic activities. A familiar spirit, who is aware that Saul's anointing has been lifted, and who is aware of the desolate state of his spiritual life, communicates with the familiar spirit who had been assigned to the prophet Samuel. The two decide that their plan to put another stake in Saul's prophetic coffin would be to impersonate Samuel, which would be a simple diabolical endeavor because the spirit assigned to him would know everything about him, right down to his deportment, decorum, persona, and unique physiological characteristics. A familiar spirit of one person can communicate with the familiar spirit of another person. That is why, in the instance of abuse, the abused can be in another city or state and feel the presence of the abuser, who can pick up his activities and whereabouts. This is because they form strong lines of communication between themselves. When there is a covenant made, it is not only made between the persons, but also the between the familiar spirits assigned to them. They form attachments in the realm of the spirit, which are often difficult

to break. You should never establish any kind of association with anyone or institution without first getting a
green light from the Father.

Familiar spirits know the person to whom they are
assigned so well that they can even imitate them. This
ability produces the deceptive element in seance. People
are often convinced that the diviner is talking and com-
muning with their dead relatives or loved ones. These are
not dead relatives but very evil spirits, attempting to hold
them captive in the darkness of their underworld activities. The Bible warns us against establishing any kind
of communication with familiar spirits. Leviticus 19:31
clearly tells us not to regard "them that have familiar
spirits, neither seek after wizards, to be defiled by them:
I am the LORD your God." I believe Saul was aware of
this commandment. To go as undetected as one who
ignores a commandment of God, Saul attempted to hide
his real identity by camouflaging himself. As you read the
account of his rendezvous experience with the witch of
Endor, you will notice that the familiar spirit knew who
he was in spite of his masquerade. First Samuel 28:3–25
gives us further insight to the activities of familiar spirits.
As you read this account, please observe the following:

- Samuel is dead.

- The witch sees "gods" ascending out of the earth
  (regions of the underworld—see *The Rules of
  Engagement, Vol. 1: The Art of Strategic Prayer
  and Spiritual Warfare*). These are actual familiar
  (demonic) spirits disguising themselves as Samuel.

- The response of Saul was fear. Second Timothy 1:7
  states that God does not give you the spirit of fear.

Now Samuel was dead, and all Israel had lamented him, and buried him in Ramah, even in his own city. And Saul had put away those that had familiar spirits, and the wizards, out of the land. And the Philistines gathered themselves together, and came and pitched in Shunem: and Saul gathered all Israel together, and they pitched in Gilboa. And when Saul saw the host of the Philistines, he was afraid, and his heart greatly trembled. And when Saul enquired of the LORD, the LORD answered him not, neither by dreams nor by Urim, nor by prophets. Then said Saul unto his servants, Seek me a woman that hath a familiar spirit, that I may go to her, and inquire of her. And his servants said to him, Behold, there is a woman that hath a familiar spirit at Endor. And Saul disguised himself, and put on other raiment, and he went, and two men with him, and they came to the woman by night: and he said, I pray thee, divine unto me by the familiar spirit, and bring me him up, whom I shall name unto thee. And the woman said unto him, Behold, thou knowest what Saul hath done, how he hath cut off those that have familiar spirits, and the wizards, out of the land: wherefore then layest thou a snare for my life, to cause me to die? And Saul sware to her by the LORD, saying, As the LORD liveth, there shall no punishment happen to thee for this thing. Then said the woman, Whom shall I bring up unto thee? And he said, Bring me up Samuel. And when the woman saw Samuel, she cried with a loud voice: and the woman spake to Saul, saying, Why hast thou deceived me? for thou art Saul. And the king said unto her, Be not afraid: for what sawest thou? And the woman said unto Saul, I saw gods ascending out of the earth. And he said unto her, What form is he of? And she said, An old man cometh up; and he is covered with a mantle. And Saul perceived that it was Samuel, and he stooped with his face to the ground, and bowed himself. And Samuel said to Saul, Why hast thou disquieted me, to bring me up? And Saul answered, I am sore distressed; for the Philistines make war against me, and God is departed from me, and answereth me no more, neither by prophets, nor by dreams: therefore I have called thee, that thou mayest make known unto me what I shall do. Then said Samuel, Wherefore then dost thou ask of me, seeing the LORD is departed from thee, and is become thine enemy? And the LORD hath done to him, as he spake by me: for the LORD hath rent the kingdom out of thine hand, and given it to thy neighbour, even to David: Because thou obeyedst not the voice of the LORD, nor executedst his fierce wrath upon Amalek, therefore hath the LORD done this thing unto thee this day. Moreover the LORD will also deliver Israel with thee into the hand of the Philistines: and to morrow shalt thou and thy sons be with me: the LORD also shall deliver the host of Israel into the hand of the Philistines. Then Saul fell straightway all along on the earth, and was sore afraid, because of the words of Samuel: and there was no strength in him; for he had eaten no bread all the day, nor all the night. And the woman came unto Saul, and saw that he was sore troubled, and said unto him, Behold, thine handmaid hath obeyed thy voice, and I have put my life in my hand, and have hearkened unto thy words which thou spakest unto me. Now therefore, I pray thee, hearken thou also unto the voice of thine handmaid, and let me set a morsel of bread before thee; and eat, that thou mayest have strength, when thou goest on thy way. But he refused, and said, I will not eat. But his servants, together with the woman, compelled him; and he hearkened unto their voice. So he arose from the earth, and sat upon the bed. And the woman had a fat calf in the house; and she hasted, and killed it, and took flour, and kneaded it, and did bake unleavened bread thereof: And she brought it before Saul, and before his servants; and they did eat. Then they rose up, and went away that night.

—1 SAMUEL 28:3–25

Familiar spirits form confederations; tracking activities of men and women of God, divine visitations and kingdom initiatives through religious spirits as well. Matthew 28:1–13, records the following account:

In the end of the Sabbath, as it began to dawn toward the first day of the week, came Mary Magdalene and the other Mary to see the sepulchre. And, behold, there was a great earthquake: for the angel of the Lord descended from heaven, and came and rolled back the stone from the door, and sat upon it. His countenance was like lightning, and his raiment white as snow: And for fear of him the keepers did shake, and became as dead men. And the angel answered and said unto the women, Fear not ye: for I know that ye seek Jesus, which was crucified. He is not here: for he is risen, as he said. Come, see the place where the Lord lay. And go quickly, and tell his disciples that he is risen from the dead; and, behold, he goeth before you into Galilee; there shall ye see him: lo, I have told you. And they departed quickly from the sepulchre with fear and great joy; and did run to bring his disciples word. And as they went to tell his disciples, behold, Jesus met them, saying, All hail. And they came and held him by the feet, and worshipped him. Then said Jesus unto them, Be not afraid: go tell my brethren that they go into Galilee, and there shall they see me. Now when they were going, behold, some of the watch came into the city, and shewed unto the chief priests all the things that were done. And when they were assembled with the elders, and had taken counsel, they gave large money unto the soldiers, Saying, Say ye, His disciples came by night, and stole him away while we slept.

Acts 16:16–21 records another instance. In this text we read of a young woman who was able to work with familiar spirits. The intent was to discredit Paul's ministry by deceiving the people, causing them to believe that he was associated with her:

And it came to pass, as we went to prayer, a certain damsel possessed with a spirit of divination met us, which brought her masters much gain by soothsaying: The same followed Paul and us, and cried, saying, These men are the servants of the most high God, which shew unto us the way of salvation. And this did she many days. But Paul, being grieved, turned and said to the spirit, I command thee in the name of Jesus Christ to come out of her. And he came out the same hour. And when her masters saw that the hope of their gains was gone, they caught Paul and

Silas, and drew them into the marketplace unto the rulers, And brought them to the magistrates, saying, These men, being Jews, do exceedingly trouble our city, And teach customs, which are not lawful for us to receive, neither to observe, being Romans.

Familiar spirits know your "hot spots." They know which buttons to push. They know your:

- Weaknesses
- Strengths
- Dislikes
- Likes
- Passions
- Pet peeves
- What gets you going
- What upsets you
- What distracts you
- Desires
- Ambitions…
- Everything!

Familiar spirits have:

- Geographical assignments (Mark 5:1–10)
- Cultural assignments (Num. 33:50–55)
- Individual assignments (1 Samuel 28:3–9; 1 Chron. 10:13)

To accomplish their goals and purpose, they can use:

- Animals (i.e. black cats, frogs)

- Talisman (any object, or piece of clothing that witches and warlocks and other workers of the craft use to transfer spells and hexes)

- People whose lives are characterized by demonic/satanic alliances

Familiar spirits act as informants to a larger network of demons who function as a kind of satanic intelligence. (See Daniel 11:30.) Their portfolios include their roles as informants and council to Satan, and other highly specialized principalities, powers, or rulers of the darkness of this world. I can imagine them reporting to satanic councils, bringing to the table information that would be utilized in the designing of attacks and strongholds, and the creating of weapons of mass destructions designed to kill and destroy individuals, families, ministries, purpose, communities, and nations. Familiar spirits observe very strict protocols. Although they are not employed to attack, in addition to the aforementioned tasks, their job descriptions would also include the examining of spiritual hedges of protection built around believers, in an attempt to identify and locate perforations. Job 1:7–11 and 3:25 record an example of this activity. Fear created a perforation in Job's hedge, thus allowing Satan to send in his agents to steal, kill, and destroy. In fulfilling their roles as counsel to Satan, high ranking principalities, and powers, they offer suggestions to them as to how best to keep an individual in bondage. In this instance, gatekeepers and doorkeepers would be employed to allow or prohibit access to an individual, family, community, nation, organization, or ministry. Every city, country, family, person, and any living entity has gates and doors, hence Psalm 24:7–10: "Lift up your heads, O ye gates; and be ye lift up, ye everlasting doors; and the King of glory shall come in. Who is this King of glory? The LORD strong and mighty, the LORD mighty in battle. Lift up your heads, O ye gates; even lift them up, ye everlasting doors; and the King of glory shall come in. Who is this King of glory? The LORD of hosts, he is the King of glory. Selah."

Concerning you as a human being, you have three gates and seventeen doors to your soul and body that provide portals through which spirits enter. They are as follows:

# Gates

- Lust of the Flesh
- Lust of the Eyes
- Pride of Life

# Doors

- Olfactory (2)
- Visual (2)
- Auditory (2)
- Kinesthetic (1)
- Gustatory (2)
- Reproductive/Sexual (4)
- Motion and Movement (2)
- Action and Accomplishments (2)

Make God the Father, God the Son, and God the Holy Spirit your new Gate and Doorkeeper.

### 3. Spirits of inheritance and generational curses

Biologists, sociologists, and psychologists all agree that there lies within man the propensity for certain idiosyncratic behaviors, tendencies, traits, weaknesses, strengths, and habits peculiar to particular families. These things, they say, are passed down by the programming of the DNA. According to Exodus 20:5 God says, "I the LORD thy God am a jealous God, visiting the iniquity of the fathers upon the children unto the third and fourth generation of them that hate me." This scripture passage lets us know that we are dealing with intergenerational spirits, which are responsible for producing:

- Family and community peculiarities
- Ancestral eccentricities
- Idiosyncratic issues
- Ethnic traits
- Social tendencies
- Clannish oddities
- Pathological conditions of the mind and body
- Individualities
- Fundamental values
- Cultures
- Passions
- Motives
- Intentions
- Agendas
- Habits
- Ideologies
- Perceptions
- Temperaments
- Personalities
- Illnesses
- Degenerative diseases
- Congenital diseases

## 4. Unholy alliances: diabolical confederations and associations

Satan, a master strategist and tactician, employs principalities and spirits whose special assignment is to identify and mobilize other principalities and spirits to form confederations. They may be configured as legions as with the Gadarene in Mark 5:1–20, or use entire communities, nations, or individuals in order to accomplish their heinous mandates and insidious assignments such as the mob in Acts 16:12–24. What is *not* important to these spirits is the *ethos*, purpose, mission, or differences of any groupings of spirits or people as separate entities. What *is* important is the ultimate fulfillment of their diabolical goals that the incited confederation will accomplish. They are no respecter of persons. Unholy alliances can take on the form of:

- Spirit to spirit
- Spirit to soul
- Spirit to body
- Body to body
- Soul to body

This kind of satanic activity can either take on the form of total possession when the identity, personality, and the will of a spirit-being is superimposed upon the identity, personality, and will of the host, or influence from without. In this case you will have suppression, oppression, and repression. They affect humanity:

# Spiritually

- Mind
- Will
- Destiny
- Purpose
- Gifts
- Ability
- Conviction
- Belief System

- Value
- Culture
- Ethics

## Psychologically

- Emotion
- Personality
- Temperament
- Unconscious behavior and activity
- Perception

## Neurologically

- Frontal lobe
- Behavior
- Abstract thought processes
- Problem solving
- Attention
- Creative thought
- Some emotion
- Intellect
- Reflection
- Judgment
- Initiative
- Inhibition
- Coordination of movement
- Generalized and mass movement
- Some eye movement
- Sense of smell
- Muscle movement
- Skilled movement
- Some motor skill
- Physical reaction
- Libido (sexual urge)

# Occipital Lobe

- Vision
- Reading

# Parietal Lobe

- Sense of touch (tactile sensation)
- Appreciation of form through touch (stereognosis)
- Response to internal stimuli (proprioception)
- Sensory combination and comprehension
- Some language and reading functions
- Some visual functions

# Temporal Lobe

- Auditory memory
- Some hearing
- Visual memory
- Some vision, pathway
- Other memory
- Music
- Fear
- Some language
- Some speech
- Some behavior and emotion
- Sense of identity

# Right Hemisphere (Representational Hemisphere)

- Control of the left side of the body
- Temporal and spatial relationships
- Analyze nonverbal information

- Communicate emotions
- Creativity

# Left Hemisphere
# (Categorical Hemisphere)

- Logic ability
- Control of the right side of the body
- Produce and understand language
- Communicate between the left and right side of the brain

## Corpus Callosum

- Connects right and left hemispheres
- Communication between the left and right hemispheres

## The Cerebellum

- Balance
- Posture
- Cardiac, respiratory, and vasomotor centers

## The Brain Stem

- Motor and sensory pathway to body and face
- Vital centers: cardiac, respiratory, vasomotor (heartbeat, breathing, blood pressure)

## Hypothalamus

- Mood
- Motivation
- Sexual maturation

- Temperature regulation
- Hormonal body process

# Thalamus

- Sensory motor functions

# Optic Chasm

- Vision and the optic nerve

# Pituitary Gland

- Hormonal body process
- Physical maturation
- Growth (height and form)
- Sexual maturation
- Sexual functioning

# Spinal Cord

- Conduit and source of sensation and movement

# Pineal Body

- Unknown, but new-agers call this the "third-eye"

# Reticular Formation

- Internal dialogue

# Limbic System

- Olfactory
- Emotion
- Motivation

- Behavior
- Various autonomic function
- Communication between left and right brain

In the case of possession, it is possible for all the above areas to be affected. An example of this was Nebucaddazar. Daniel 5:18–21 states, "O thou king, the most high God gave Nebuchadnezzar thy father a kingdom, and majesty, and glory, and honour: And for the majesty that he gave him, all people, nations, and languages, trembled and feared before him: whom he would he slew; and whom he would he kept alive; and whom he would he set up; and whom he would he put down. But when his heart was lifted up, and his mind hardened in pride, he was deposed from his kingly throne, and they took his glory from him: And he was driven from the sons of men; and his heart was made like the beasts, and his dwelling was with the wild asses: they fed him with grass like oxen, and his body was wet with the dew of heaven; till he knew that the most high God ruled in the kingdom of men, and that he appointeth over it whomsoever he will."

## Unholy Alliances Produce:

- Strongholds
- Imaginations
- High things
- Ambitions
- Desires
- Bondages
- Habits
- Soul ties
- Attachments
- Entanglements

- Affinities
- Weights
- Besetting sin
- Snares
- Stumbling blocks
- Yokes
- Covenants
- A variety of intrinsic and extrinsic weapons

# Categories

### *Demons, principalities, and spirits with other demons, principalities, and spirits*

For we wrestle not against flesh and blood, but against principalities, against powers, against the rulers of the darkness of this world, against spiritual wickedness in high places.

—EPHESIANS 6:12

### *Demons, principalities, and spirits with organizations*

And when they were assembled with the elders, and had taken counsel, they gave large money unto the soldiers, Saying, Say ye, His disciples came by night, and stole him away while we slept. And if this come to the governor's ears, we will persuade him, and secure you. So they took the money, and did as they were taught: and this saying is commonly reported among the Jews until this day.

—MATTHEW 28:12–15

## *Demons, principalities, and spirits with groups of people*

> When they heard these things, they were cut to the heart, and they gnashed on him with their teeth. But he, being full of the Holy Ghost, looked up stedfastly into heaven, and saw the glory of God, and Jesus standing on the right hand of God, And said, Behold, I see the heavens opened, and the Son of man standing on the right hand of God. Then they cried out with a loud voice, and stopped their ears, and ran upon him with one accord, And cast him out of the city, and stoned him.
>
> —ACTS 7:54–58

## *Demons, principalities, and spirits with nations*

> Keep not thou silence, O God: hold not thy peace, and be not still, O Go. For, lo, thine enemies make a tumult: and they that hate thee have lifted up the head. They have taken crafty counsel against thy people, and consulted against thy hidden ones. They have said, Come, and let us cut them off from being a nation; that the name of Israel may be no more in remembrance. For they have consulted together with one consent: they are confederate against thee: The tabernacles of Edom, and the Ishmaelites; of Moab, and the Hagarenes; Gebal, and Ammon, and Amalek; the Philistines with the inhabitants of Tyre; Assur also is joined with them: they have holpen the children of Lot. Selah.
>
> —PSALM 83:1–8

## *Demons, principalities, and spirits with believers*

And there was great joy in that city. But there was a certain man, called Simon, which beforetime in the same city used sorcery, and bewitched the people of Samaria, giving out that himself was some great one: To whom they all gave heed, from the least to the greatest, saying, This man is the great power of God. And to him they had regard, because that of long time he had bewitched them with sorceries. But when they believed Philip preaching the things concerning the kingdom of God, and the name of Jesus Christ, they were baptized, both men and women. Then Simon himself believed also: and when he was baptized, he continued with Philip, and wondered, beholding the miracles and signs which were done. Now when the apostles which were at Jerusalem heard that Samaria had received the word of God, they sent unto them Peter and John: Who, when they were come down, prayed for them, that they might receive the Holy Ghost: (For as yet he was fallen upon none of them: only they were baptized in the name of the Lord Jesus.) Then laid they their hands on them, and they received the Holy Ghost. And when Simon saw that through laying on of the apostles' hands the Holy Ghost was given, he offered them money, Saying, Give me also this power, that on whomsoever I lay hands, he may receive the Holy Ghost. But Peter said unto him, Thy money perish with thee, because thou hast thought that the gift of God may be purchased with money. Thou hast neither part nor lot in this matter: for thy heart is not right in the sight of God. Repent therefore of this thy wickedness, and pray God, if perhaps the thought of thine heart may be forgiven thee. For I perceive that thou art in the gall of bitterness, and in the bond of iniquity. Then answered Simon, and said, Pray ye to the Lord for me, that none of these things which ye have spoken come upon me. And they, when they had testified and preached the word of the Lord, returned to Jerusalem, and preached the gospel in many villages of the Samaritans.

—ACTS 8:8–25

And Jesus said unto him, Forbid him not: for he that is not against us is for us. And it came to pass, when the time was come that he should be received up, he stedfastly set his face to go to Jerusalem, And sent messengers before his face: and they went, and entered into a village of the Samaritans, to make ready for him. And they did not receive him, because his face was as though he would go to Jerusalem. And when his disciples James and John saw this, they said, Lord, wilt thou that we command fire to come down from heaven, and consume them, even as Elias did? But he turned, and rebuked them, and said, Ye know not what manner of spirit ye are of. For the Son of man is not come to destroy men's lives, but to save them. And they went to another village.

—LUKE 9:50–56

## Demons, principalities, and spirits with satanic representatives

And I saw three unclean spirits like frogs come out of the mouth of the dragon, and out of the mouth of the beast, and out of the mouth of the false prophet. For they are the spirits of devils, working miracles, which go forth unto the kings of the earth and of the whole world, to gather them to the battle of that great day of God Almighty.

—REVELATION 16:13–14

### Demons, principalities, and spirits with heads of state

Possession, oppression, influence through confederations, associations, covenants, and pacts (such as Hitler or Stalin).

The word of the LORD came again unto me, saying, Son of man, say unto the prince of Tyrus, Thus saith the Lord GOD; Because thine heart is lifted up, and thou hast said, I am a God, I sit in the seat of God, in the midst of the seas; yet thou art a man, and not God, though thou set thine heart as the heart of God: Behold, thou art wiser than Daniel; there is no secret that they can hide from thee: With thy wisdom and with thine understanding thou hast gotten thee riches, and hast gotten gold and silver into thy treasures: By thy great wisdom and by thy traffick hast thou increased thy riches, and thine heart is lifted up because of thy riches: Therefore thus saith the Lord GOD; Because thou hast set thine heart as the heart of God; Behold, therefore I will bring strangers upon thee, the terrible of the nations: and they shall draw their swords against the beauty of thy wisdom, and they shall defile thy brightness. They shall bring thee down to the pit, and thou shalt die the deaths of them that are slain in the midst of the seas. Wilt thou yet say before him that slayeth thee, I am God? but thou shalt be a man, and no God, in the hand of him that slayeth thee. Thou shalt die the deaths of the uncircumcised by the hand of strangers: for I have spoken it, saith the Lord GOD. Moreover the word of the LORD came unto me, saying, Son of man, take up a lamentation upon the king of Tyrus, and say unto him, Thus saith the Lord GOD; Thou sealest up the sum, full of wisdom, and perfect in beauty. Thou hast been in Eden the garden of God; every precious stone was thy covering, the sardius, topaz, and the diamond, the beryl, the onyx, and the jasper, the sapphire, the emerald, and the carbuncle, and gold: the workmanship of thy tabrets and of thy pipes was prepared in thee in the day that thou wast created. Thou art the anointed cherub that covereth; and I have set thee so: thou wast upon the holy mountain of God; thou hast walked up and down in the midst of the stones of fire. Thou wast perfect in thy ways from the day that thou wast created, till iniquity was found in thee. By the multitude of thy merchandise they have filled the midst of thee with violence, and thou hast sinned: therefore I will cast thee as profane out of the mountain of God: and I will destroy thee, O covering cherub, from the midst of the stones of fire. Thine heart was lifted up because of thy beauty, thou hast corrupted thy wisdom by reason of thy brightness: I will cast thee to the ground, I will lay thee before kings, that they may behold thee. Thou hast defiled thy sanctuaries by the multitude of thine iniquities, by the iniquity of thy traffick; therefore will I bring forth a fire from the midst of thee, it shall devour thee, and I will bring thee to ashes upon the earth in the sight of all them that behold thee. All they that know thee among the people shall be astonished at thee: thou shalt be a terror, and never shalt thou be any more.

—EZEKIEL 28:1–19

## *Demons, principalities, and spirits with governments and political regimes*

It pleased Darius to set over the kingdom an hundred and twenty princes, which should be over the whole kingdom; And over these three presidents; of whom Daniel was first: that the princes might give accounts unto them, and the king should have no damage. Then this Daniel was preferred above the presidents and princes, because an excellent spirit was in him; and the king thought to set him over the whole realm. Then the presidents and princes sought to find occasion against Daniel concerning the kingdom; but they could find none occasion nor fault; forasmuch as he was faithful, neither was there any error or fault found in him. Then said these men, We shall not find any occasion against this Daniel, except we find it against him concerning the law of his God. Then these presidents and princes assembled together to the king, and said thus unto him, King Darius, live for ever. All the presidents of the kingdom, the governors, and the princes, the counselors, and the captains, have consulted together to establish a royal statute, and to make a firm decree, that whosoever shall ask a petition of any God or man for thirty days, save of thee, O king, he shall be cast into the den of lions. Now, O king, establish the decree, and sign the writing, that it be not changed, according to the law of the

Medes and Persians, which altereth not. Wherefore king Darius signed the writing and the decree. Now when Daniel knew that the writing was signed, he went into his house; and his windows being open in his chamber toward Jerusalem, he kneeled upon his knees three times a day, and prayed, and gave thanks before his God, as he did aforetime.

—DANIEL 6:1–10

At the time appointed he shall return, and come toward the south; but it shall not be as the former, or as the latter. For the ships of Chittim shall come against him: therefore he shall be grieved, and return, and have indignation against the holy covenant: so shall he do; he shall even return, and have intelligence with them that forsake the holy covenant. And arms shall stand on his part, and they shall pollute the sanctuary of strength, and shall take away the daily sacrifice, and they shall place the abomination that maketh desolate. And such as do wickedly against the covenant shall he corrupt by flatteries: but the people that do know their God shall be strong, and do exploits. And they that understand among the people shall instruct many: yet they shall fall by the sword, and by flame, by captivity, and by spoil, many days.

—DANIEL 11:29–33

But it came to pass, that when Sanballat heard that we builded the wall, he was wroth, and took great indignation, and mocked the Jews. And he spake before his brethren and the army of Samaria, and said, what do these feeble Jews? will they fortify themselves? will they sacrifice? will they make an end in a day? will they revive the stones out of the heaps of the rubbish which are burned? Now Tobiah the Ammonite was by him, and he said, Even that which they build, if a fox go up, he shall even break down their stone wall....Then said I unto them, Ye see the distress that we are in, how Jerusalem lieth waste, and the gates thereof are burned with fire: come, and let us build up the wall of Jerusalem, that we be no more a reproach. Then I told them of the hand of my God, which was good upon me; as also the king's words that he had spoken unto me. And they said, Let us rise up and build. So they strengthened their hands for this good work. But when Sanballat the Horonite, and Tobiah the servant, the Ammonite, and Geshem the Arabian, heard it, they laughed us to scorn, and despised us, and said, What is this thing that ye do? will ye rebel against the king?

—NEHEMIAH 4:1–3; 2:17–19

## *Demons, principalities, and spirits with nonbelievers*

When they heard these things, they were cut to the heart, and they gnashed on him with their teeth. But he, being full of the Holy Ghost, looked up stedfastly into heaven, and saw the glory of God, and Jesus standing on the right hand of God. And said, Behold, I see the heavens opened, and the Son of man standing on the right hand of God. Then they cried out with a loud voice, and stopped their ears, and ran upon him with one accord. And cast him out of the city, and stoned him: and the witnesses laid down their clothes at a young man's feet, whose name was Saul. And they stoned Stephen, calling upon God, and saying Lord Jesus, receive my spirit. And he kneeled down, and cried with a loud voice, Lord, lay not this sin to their charge. And when he had said this he fell asleep.

—ACTS 7:54–60

## *People with people*

But king Solomon loved many strange women, together with the daughter of Pharaoh, women of the Moabites, Ammonites, Edomites, Zidonians, and Hittites; Of the nations concerning which the LORD said unto the children of Israel, Ye shall not go in to them, neither shall they come in unto you: for surely they will turn away your heart after their gods: Solomon clave unto these in love. And he had seven hundred wives, princesses, and three hundred concubines: and his wives turned away his heart. For it came to pass, when Solomon was old, that his wives turned away his heart after other gods: and his heart was not perfect with the LORD his God, as was the heart of David his father. For Solomon went after Ashtoreth the goddess of the Zidonians, and after Milcom the abomination of the Ammonites.

—1 KINGS 11:1–5

Know ye not that your bodies are the members of Christ? shall I then take the members of Christ, and make them the members of an harlot? God forbid. What? know ye not that he which is joined to an harlot is one body? for two, saith he, shall be one flesh.

—1 CORINTHIANS 6:15–16

All of the above categories affect the:

- mind
- will
- emotion
- perception
- belief
- conviction
- temperament
- personality

| Signs, Symptoms, and Manifestations of the Spirit of Affinity | | |
| --- | --- | --- |
| Irritations | Vexations | Stirrings |
| Frustrations | Temptations | Harassments |
| Accusations | Perversions | Impressions |
| Concentrations/focus | Interceptions | Provocations |
| Negotiations | Contentions | Prohibitions |
| Deceptions | Inhibitions | Alterations |
| Persecutions | Relations | Subversions |
| Insinuations | Illusions | Disillusions |
| Projections | Suspicions | Manipulations |
| Deprivation | Desolation | Oppression |
| Depression | Misrepresentations | Justifications |
| Misinformation | Conclusions | Dysfunctions |
| Addictions | Distortions | Rationalizations |
| Afflictions | Attractions | Speculations |
| Satanic operations | Stigmas | Family secrets |
| Divination | Seduction | Decisions |

| | | |
|---|---|---|
| Resolutions | Associations | Psychosis |
| Dreams | Disillusions | Nightmares |
| Psychosis | Neurosis | Assaults |
| Alliances | Insults | Slanders |
| Burdens | Discouragements | Confusion |
| Divisions | Interference | Snares |
| Entanglements | Misunderstandings | Denial |
| Rulings | Resistance | Diseases |
| Ailments | Defects | Disabilities |
| Disorders | Infections | Infirmities |
| Bands | Connections | Contaminations |
| Victimization | Inordinate affections | Enmeshments |
| Mishaps | Stigmas | Misfortunes |
| Fantasies | Impure motives | Strange occurrences |
| Glass ceilings | Unexplainable accidents | Lusts |
| Hidden agendas | Character assassinations | Questionable motives |
| Unethical behavior | Strongholds | High things |
| Ungodly ambitions | Unholy desires | Bondages |
| Habits | Affinities | Weights |
| Besetting sin | Stumbling blocks | Knowledge blocks |
| Yokes | Covenants | Vitiation of will |
| Repression of memories | Insomnia | Satanic barriers |
| Perverted imaginations | Suppression of emotions | Perversions of thoughts |

| Calcification of the heart | Diabolical proclivities and appetites | Neurotic and psychotic behaviors and tendencies |
|---|---|---|
| Attachments (include the use of talisman, books, clothing, furniture, jewelry) | | |

**Release:** Pursue an intimate personal relationship with the Lord (see Psalm 42:1); declarations from the book series *The Rules of Engagement.*

# Spirit of Affliction

AFFLICTIONS ARE THE pathological conditions of the body, soul, or spirit. This word comes from the Hebrew word *ra,* which literally translated means "to break into pieces or to devour." It connotes a spirit that is assigned to cause distress, disease, and to ultimately destroy. The spirit of affliction works with all major maladies and calamities. Psalm 34:19 states, "Many are the afflictions of the righteous: but the LORD delivereth him out of them all." The following is a list of categories:

## Physical

- Nervous
- Integumentary
- Respiratory
- Muscular
- Digestive
- Skeletal
- Reproductive
- Endocrine

- Circulatory
- Urinary

# Mental/Psychological

- Nightmares
- Night terrors
- Phobias
- Depression
- Mental illness
- Oppression
- Possession
- Poor memory
- Inefficient recall
- Guilt-tripping
- Insomnia
- Excessive self-analysis
- Polarized emotions
- Filthy thoughts
- Unclean fantasies

# Financial

- Deprivation
- Lack
- Debt
- Poverty
- Gambling Addiction

# Domestic/Familial

- Divorces
- Family Secrets
- Abuse
- Incest

- Competition
- Arguments

# Emotional

- Loneliness
- Depression
- Suppression
- Repression
- Rejection
- Disillusionment
- Discouragement
- Emotional instability
- Unforgiveness
- Bitterness

# Social

- Prejudice
- Harassment
- Rejection
- Alienation
- Isolation

# Biological

- Cardiovascular
- Excretory
- Gastrointestinal
- Hormonal (biochemical)
- Neurological (bioelectrical)
- Reproductive
- Respiratory
- Immunological
- Musculoskeletal

## Physiological

Demon spirits will attempt to create physiologcal afflictions, which lead to the malfunctioning of normal processes in the body.

- Aches
- Pain
- Swelling
- Bleeding
- Growths
- Infection
- Itching
- Movement disorder
- Sickness
- Disease
- Fatigue

## Emotional

- Fear
- Guilt
- Shame
- Anger
- Worry
- Unforgiveness
- Revenge
- Bitterness

# Nutritional

- High fat
- High sodium
- Yo-yo dieting
- Feasting-Fasting Syndrome

**Release:** Healing to: mind, body, soul, spirit; finances, prosperity, success, aligning to biblical principles and dietary laws, miracles, signs and wonders, wisdom, budgeting, inspiration, counsel, might, patience, the will of God, hope, faith, salvation, forgiveness from God for sin, backsliding, misuse of tongue, resentment, pride, impenitence, mistreatment of others, hardness of the heart, idolatry, and hypocrisy.

# Spirit of Ahab
## (Codependency)

THIS SPIRIT WORKS in conjunction with the Jezebel Spirit. When warring against this spirit, you must also tackle the spirit of Jezebel as well. The individual operating under the influence of the spirit of Ahab complies with wishes, commands and directives given by those influenced or possessed by the Jezebel spirit, even when it goes against their own personal will and conviction. This spirit undermines a person's rights, and authority, and totally opens them to be disrespected and to have their boundaries violated, be they territorial, personal, or psychological. This spirit is a doorkeeper, and its discretion opens doors to other principalities and strongholds.

Codependency is a common family problem. It is a dysfunction in which a person lets someone else's behavior affect them, and who are obsessed with controlling that person's behavior, emotions, perceptions, lifestyle and actions. They are so preoccupied with rescuing and helping others with their problems that they ignore what's happening inside themselves. It is an adaptation to stress that causes imbalance within a family. The primary stressor will usually be addicted to alcohol, drugs, food, shopping, gambling, sex, violence, work, and negativism. As long as the stress exists, members of the family attempt to bring balance. Some assume the role of "hero," "scapegoat," or "comedian." They gain relief by diverting attention from the real problem and not attracting attention to self. Individuals caught up in this syndrome usually project themselves as "the perfect child," the "surrogate parent/spouse," etc. When children grow up, they continue to play roles until sometimes it becomes destructive.

Codependent people are easy to spot. They either try to control others and get angry and retreat when others refuse their "help," saying, "I'm just trying to help," or "You'll wish you took my help," or "If you don't want me someone else will." Or they take on the role of always needing help and assistance. They have learned rescuing and survival strategies, a behavior from dysfunctional relationships that are characterized by manipulation and control. They are also "clingy," and smothering.

| Signs, Symptoms, and Manifestations of the Spirit of Ahab | | |
|---|---|---|
| Fear of authority figures | Disillusionment | Fear of rejection |
| Confusion | Discouragement | Depression |
| Excessive self-analysis | Insomnia | Intimidation |
| Oppression | Inertia | Rejection syndrome |

| Lack of self-expression | Guilt-tripping | Suppression |
|---|---|---|
| Poor memory | Inefficient recall | Blind obedience |
| Idolatry | Cowardice | Compromise |
| Repression | Insecurity | Not feeling well |
| Suicidal tendency | Alienation | Self-blame |
| Martyr syndrome | Fear of retaliation | Poor me/why me |
| Psychic manipulation | Worry/anxiety | Demonic slavery |
| Religious martyr | Lost little boy/girl syndrome | Dependent personality |
| Immorality upon request/force/coercion | Physical weariness/fatigue | |

**Release:** Peace, self-control, righteousness, love, boldness, sound mind, call on Jehovah Adonai, purpose, hope, maturity, liberty, independence, potential, and leadership.

# Spirit of Amnon

THE SPIRIT OF Amnon, through lust and the employment of devious strategies, perpetuates incest within a family line. This powerful spirit can lie dormant and go undiscovered for years. It acts as a doorkeeper to spirits of affinity, perversion, and a host of other spirits that undermine the sanctity of the family, marriage, and the home. **Incest** is sexual activity between nuclear and extended family members, which not only include parents with children and sexual relations among siblings, but also cousins, uncles, aunts, step-parents, and grandparents. An insidious spirit, which establishes a strong confederation with the appetites of the soul, will stop at nothing until its lustful desires are satisfied. It does not allow the host to be constrained by convictions, internal mechanisms of right and wrong, and will often lead its host to justify or rationalize its actions.

And it came to pass after this, that Absalom the son of David had a fair sister, whose name was Tamar; and Amnon the son of David loved her. And Amnon

was so vexed, that he fell sick for his sister Tamar;
for she was a virgin; and Amnon thought it hard for
him to do anything to her. But Amnon had a friend,
whose name was Jonadab, the son of Shimeah David's
brother: and Jonadab was a very subtil man. And he
said unto him, Why art thou, being the king's son, lean
from day to day? wilt thou not tell me? And Amnon
said unto him, I love Tamar, my brother Absalom's
sister. And Jonadab said unto him, Lay thee down on
thy bed, and make thyself sick: and when thy father
cometh to see thee, say unto him, I pray thee, let my
sister Tamar come, and give me meat, and dress the
meat in my sight, that I may see it, and eat it at her
hand. So Amnon lay down, and made himself sick:
and when the king was come to see him, Amnon said
unto the king, I pray thee, let Tamar my sister come,
and make me a couple of cakes in my sight, that I may
eat at her hand. Then David sent home to Tamar, saying, Go now to thy brother Amnon's house, and dress
him meat. So Tamar went to her brother Amnon's
house; and he was laid down. And she took flour,
and kneaded it, and made cakes in his sight, and did
bake the cakes. And she took a pan, and poured them
out before him; but he refused to eat. And Amnon
said, Have out all men from me. And they went out
every man from him. And Amnon said unto Tamar,
Bring the meat into the chamber, that I may eat of
thine hand. And Tamar took the cakes which she had
made, and brought them into the chamber to Amnon
her brother. And when she had brought them unto
him to eat, he took hold of her, and said unto her,
Come lie with me, my sister. And she answered him,
Nay, my brother, do not force me; for no such thing

ought to be done in Israel: do not thou this folly. And I, whither shall I cause my shame to go? and as for thee, thou shalt be as one of the fools in Israel. Now therefore, I pray thee, speak unto the king; for he will not withhold me from thee. Howbeit he would not hearken unto her voice: but, being stronger than she, forced her, and lay with her. Then Amnon hated her exceedingly; so that the hatred wherewith he hated her was greater than the love wherewith he had loved her. And Amnon said unto her, Arise, be gone. And she said unto him, There is no cause: this evil in sending me away is greater than the other that thou didst unto me. But he would not hearken unto her. Then he called his servant that ministered unto him, and said, Put now this woman out from me, and bolt the door after her. And she had a garment of divers colours upon her: for with such robes were the king's daughters that were virgins apparelled. Then his servant brought her out, and bolted the door after her. And Tamar put ashes on her head, and rent her garment of divers colours that was on her, and laid her hand on her head, and went on crying. And Absalom her brother said unto her, Hath Amnon thy brother been with thee? but hold now thy peace, my sister: he is thy brother; regard not this thing. So Tamar remained desolate in her brother Absalom's house. But when king David heard of all these things, he was very wroth. And Absalom spake unto his brother Amnon neither good nor bad: for Absalom hated Amnon, because he had forced his sister Tamar.

—2 SAMUEL 13:1–22

| Signs, Symptoms, and Manifestation of the Spirit Amnon | | |
|---|---|---|
| Rape | Violence | Affinity |
| Hatred | Disrespect | Plotting |
| Alienation | Carnality | Lust |
| Perversion | Shame | Guilt |
| Depression | Low perception of self | Condemnation |
| Manipulation | Torment | Deception |
| Denial | Sexual addictions | Death |
| Pedophilia | Dishonor | Abuse |
| Obsession | Coercion | Fear |
| Anxiety | Assault | Intimidation |
| Family Secrets | Inappropriate touching | Seduction |

**Release:** Protection, purpose, forgiveness, conviction of the Holy Spirit, holiness, righteousness, love, will of God, God- and Christ-centeredness, deliverance, and peace.

# Spirit of Ananias
## and Sapphira (Fraud)

THIS SPIRIT LURKS in the church, always ready to pounce upon the believer, especially during times of giving. Its ultimate purpose is total eradication and annihilation of individuals assigned to perpetuate the life of the church or ministry. It hides out in the anointing and disguises itself as a "willing" giver.

Motivation and opportunity are the elements that generally underlie the commission of fraud. These could take the form of:

**Economic motivation:** financial need or gain is the most common motivation for fraud. Often, persons convicted of fraud complain that they had overwhelming financial problems for which there was no legitimate recourse.

**Greed:** persons with power and authority often commit fraud and corruption because they are motivated by greed.

**Prestige or recognition:** persons may feel they deserve

more prestige or more recognition. These persons are often motivated by jealousy, revenge, anger, or pride. They often believe that they are superior to others, and that they are shrewd enough to confound and confuse others and can commit fraud and corruption without being discovered or detected.

**Moral Superiority**: persons may also be motivated by a cause or values that they feel are morally superior to those of the victim, organization or the ministry in this case. It is also important to understand that very often the perpetrator of fraud rationalizes his actions. For instance an employee accused of fraud is likely to rationalize his action by saying or believing that his low pay justifies the action or that since everybody is doing it he is also well within his right to do it.

> But a certain man named Ananias, with Sapphira his wife, sold a possession, And kept back part of the price, his wife also being privy to it, and brought a certain part, and laid it at the apostles' feet. But Peter said, Ananias, why hath Satan filled thine heart to lie to the Holy Ghost, and to keep back part of the price of the land? Whiles it remained, was it not thine own? and after it was sold, was it not in thine own power? why hast thou conceived this thing in thine heart? thou hast not lied unto men, but unto God. And Ananias hearing these words fell down, and gave up the ghost: and great fear came on all them that heard these things. And the young men arose, wound him up, and carried him out, and buried him. And it was about the space of three hours after, when his wife, not knowing what was done, came in. And Peter answered unto her,

Tell me whether ye sold the land for so much? And she said, Yea, for so much. Then Peter said unto her, How is it that ye have agreed together to tempt the Spirit of the Lord? behold, the feet of them which have buried thy husband are at the door, and shall carry thee out. Then fell she down straightway at his feet, and yielded up the ghost: and the young men came in, and found her dead, and, carrying her forth, buried her by her husband.

—ACTS 5:1–10

And the priest's custom with the people was, that, when any man offered sacrifice, the priest's servant came, while the flesh was in seething, with a flesh-hook of three teeth in his hand; And he struck it into the pan, or kettle, or caldron, or pot; all that the fleshhook brought up the priest took for himself. So they did in Shiloh unto all the Israelites that came thither. Also before they burnt the fat, the priest's servant came, and said to the man that sacrificed, Give flesh to roast for the priest; for he will not have sodden flesh of thee, but raw. And if any man said unto him, Let them not fail to burn the fat presently, and then take as much as thy soul desireth; then he would answer him, Nay; but thou shalt give it me now: and if not, I will take it by force. Wherefore the sin of the young men was very great before the LORD: for men abhorred the offering of the LORD.

—1 SAMUEL 2:13–17

## Signs, Symptoms, and Manifestations of the Spirit of Ananias/Sapphira

| | | |
|---|---|---|
| Hoarding | Lying | Greed |
| Selfishness | Hypocrisy | Misleading actions |
| Stinginess | Unbelief | Withholding |
| Deception | Failure to pay vows | Abuse/misuse |
| Failure to pay tithes | Internet fraud | Insurance fraud |
| Manipulation | Identity theft | Medical fraud |
| Insurance fraud | Financial fraud | Betrayal |
| Intentional deception | Inducement | Loss |
| Concealment | Breach of confidence | Dishonesty |
| Cunning craftiness | Surprise | Unfair practices |
| Camouflage | Corruption | Insider trading |
| Lack of accountability | Abuse of privileges | Rigging |
| Conflict of interest | Bribery | Nepotism |
| Favoritism | Embezzlement | False claims |
| False statements | Purchase for personal use | Illegal financial advantages |
| Passive-aggressive behavior | Misrepresentation of truth | Disrespect of the prophetic |
| Disrespect of the anointing | Misapplication of accounting policies | Misappropriation/ misapplication of assets |

| Recording of transaction without substances | Abuse/misuse of organization's/ business property and assets | Suppression or omission of the effects of transactions from records |
|---|---|---|
| Falsification or alteration of records or documents | | |

**Release:** The spirit of truth, giving anointing, wisdom, loyalty, obedience, fear of God, and covenant.

# Spirit of the Antichrist

WHEN WE SPEAK of the spirit of the Antichrist, we are speaking of this spirit operating on two dimensions: one in which the apostle Paul speaks of as the prevailing and pervasive mindset that is dominated by a principality; and the other, the actual embodiment of Satan himself. This spirit opposes God and anything or anyone that is godly.

He that saith he is in the light, and hateth his brother, is in darkness even until now....Little children, it is the last time: and as ye have heard that antichrist shall come, even now are there many antichrists; whereby we know that it is the last time.... And every spirit that confesseth not that Jesus Christ is come in the flesh is not of God: and this is that spirit of antichrist, whereof ye have heard that it should come; and even now already is it in the world.

—1 JOHN 2:9, 18; 4:3

Who opposeth and exalteth himself above all that is called God, or that is worshipped; so that he as God sitteth in the temple of God, shewing himself that he is God.

—2 THESSALONIANS 2:4

| Signs, Symptoms, and Manifestations of the Spirit of the Antichrist | | |
| --- | --- | --- |
| Subversion | Rebellion | Alienation |
| Sabotage | Desertion | "Cold love" |
| Deception | Division | Criticism |
| Hate | Church splits | New Age |
| Communism | Psychics | Astrology |
| Witchcraft | Humanism | Competition |
| Carnality | Religious spirit | Hypocrisy |
| Pride | Perversion | Lust |
| Counterfeit anointing | Lying wonders | Works of the flesh |
| Defiance | Idolatry | Blasphemy |
| False religion | Doctrines of devils | Love of money |
| Death | Oppression | Oppression of believers |
| Unrighteousness | Traditions | Occultisms |
| Contaminated anointing | Pride | "Satanic" miracles |
| Antagonism | Lies | Religiosity |
| Intimidation | Intolerance | Spirit of Jezebel |
| Mammon | Spirit of Babylon | Persecution of the righteous |

| Murder | Mental bondage | Masquerading as God or one of His ministers |
|--------|----------------|---------------------------------------------|
| Opposition to the power of God | | |

**Release:** Prophetic and apostolic anointing, spirit of liberty, truth, holiness, and discerning of spirits.

# Spirit of Apathy

THIS SPIRIT CAUSES a lack of interest or concern, especially concerning matters of importance. It also causes dullness in your spirit, blindness of the heart, and leanness of the soul. Apathy is responsible for the abortion of purpose and the undermining of potential.

> By the rivers of Babylon, there we sat down, yea, we wept, when we remembered Zion. We hanged our harps upon the willows in the midst thereof. For there they that carried us away captive required of us a song; and they that wasted us required of us mirth, saying, Sing us one of the songs of Zion. How shall we sing the LORD's song in a strange land?
>
> —PSALM 137:1–4

And unto the angel of the church of the Laodiceans write; These things saith the Amen, the faithful and true witness, the beginning of the creation of God; I know thy works, that thou art neither cold nor hot:

I would thou wert cold or hot. So then because thou art lukewarm, and neither cold nor hot, I will spue thee out of my mouth. Because thou sayest, I am rich, and increased with goods, and have need of nothing; and knowest not that thou art wretched, and miserable, and poor, and blind, and naked: I counsel thee to buy of me gold tried in the fire, that thou mayest be rich; and white raiment, that thou mayest be clothed, and that the shame of thy nakedness do not appear; and anoint thine eyes with eyesalve, that thou mayest see. As many as I love, I rebuke and chasten: be zealous therefore, and repent.

—REVELATION 3:14–19

## Signs, Symptoms, and Manifestations of the Spirit of Apathy

| | | |
|---|---|---|
| Slothfulness | Sadness | Disillusionment |
| Indifference | Depression | Sleepiness |
| Visionless | Gloom and doom | Stubbornness |
| Oppression | Laodicean spirit | Inattentiveness |
| Disinterest | Disregard | Unresponsiveness |
| Victimization | Insensibility | Unconcern |
| Lethargy | Listlessness | Detachment |
| Nonsupportive | Nonparticipation | Grief |
| Carnality | Lust | Irresponsibility |
| Lack of commitment | Lack of concern | Hopelessness |
| Nothing to live for | Nothing to die for | Irrational thoughts |

| Restlessness | Neurotic behavior | Persecution complex |
|---|---|---|
| Doubt | | |

**Release:** Expedience, urgency, joy, and a sense of significance, meaning, and purpose.

# Spirit of Babylon

BABYLON IS AN actual place that exists in the dimension of the spirit world. Babylon is a system of control. It has its own cosmological system, that is the exact antithesis of the kingdom of God. It has its own political system, legislative bodies, and governments just like another other physical, natural kingdom, nation, or country. Its principles, policies, and religious practices are promoted by the doctrines of man and devils, and permeate throughout the twelve systems of the universe. It is assigned to hinder, frustrate, and sabotage the fulfillment of purpose, undermine destinies, and imprison the souls of man. The spirits of behemoth, leviathan, mammon, Egypt/Pharaoh/Herod function with the spirit of Babylon, forming a strong confederation within many nations and countries, and controlling their destinies as well as the destinies of their citizenship.

Thus saith the LORD; Behold, I will raise up against Babylon, and against them that dwell in the midst of them that rise up against me, a destroying wind.

—JEREMIAH 51:1

Now the feast of unleavened bread drew nigh, which is called the Passover. And the chief priests and scribes sought how they might kill him; for they feared the people. Then entered Satan into Judas surnamed Iscariot, being of the number of the twelve. And he went his way, and communed with the chief priests and captains, how he might betray him unto them. And they were glad, and covenanted to give him money.

—LUKE 22:1–5

Then all the captains of the forces, and Johanan the son of Kareah, and Jezaniah the son of Hoshaiah, and all the people from the least even unto the greatest, came near, And said unto Jeremiah the prophet, Let, we beseech thee, our supplication be accepted before thee, and pray for us unto the LORD thy God, even for all this remnant; (for we are left but a few of many, as thine eyes do behold us:) That the LORD thy God may shew us the way wherein we may walk, and the thing that we may do. Then Jeremiah the prophet said unto them, I have heard you; behold, I will pray unto the LORD your God according to your words; and it shall come to pass, that whatsoever thing the LORD shall answer you, I will declare it unto you; I will keep nothing back from you. Then they said to Jeremiah, The LORD be a true and faithful witness between us, if we do not even according to all things for the which the LORD thy God shall send thee to us. Whether it be good, or whether it be evil, we will obey the voice of the LORD our God, to whom we send thee; that it may be well with us, when we obey the voice of the LORD our God. And it came to pass after ten days, that the word of the LORD came unto Jeremiah. Then called he Johanan the son of Kareah, and all the captains of the forces which were with him, and all the people from the least even to the greatest, And said unto them, Thus saith the LORD, the God of Israel, unto whom ye sent me to present your supplication before him; If ye will still abide in this land, then will I build you, and not pull you down, and I will plant you, and not pluck you up: for I repent me of the evil that I have done unto you. Be not afraid of the king of Babylon, of whom ye are afraid; be not afraid of him, saith the LORD: for I am with you to save you, and to deliver you from his hand. And I will shew mercies unto you, that he may have mercy upon you, and cause you to return to your own land.

—JEREMIAH 42:1–12

And the fourth angel poured out his vial upon the sun; and power was given unto him to scorch men with fire. And men were scorched with great heat, and blasphemed the name of God, which hath power over these plagues: and they repented not to give him glory. And the fifth angel poured out his vial upon the seat of the beast; and his kingdom was full of darkness; and they gnawed their tongues for pain, And blasphemed the God of heaven because of their pains and their sores, and repented not of their deeds. And the sixth angel poured out his vial upon the great river Euphrates; and the water thereof was dried up, that the way of the kings of the east might be prepared. And I saw three unclean spirits like frogs come out of the mouth of the dragon, and out of the mouth of the beast, and out of the mouth of the false prophet. For they are the spirits of devils, working miracles, which go forth unto the kings of the earth and of the whole world, to gather them to the battle of that great day of God Almighty. Behold, I come as a thief. Blessed is he that watcheth, and keepeth his garments, lest he walk naked, and they see his shame. And he gathered them together into a place called in the Hebrew tongue Armageddon. And the seventh angel poured out his vial into the air; and there came a great voice out of the temple of heaven, from the throne, saying, It is done. And there were voices, and thunders, and lightnings; and there was a great earthquake, such as was not since men were upon the earth, so mighty an earthquake, and so great. And the great city was divided into three parts, and the cities of the nations fell: and great Babylon came in remembrance before God, to give unto her the cup of the wine of the fierceness of his wrath. And every island fled away, and the mountains were not found. And there fell upon men a great hail out of heaven, every stone about the weight of a talent: and men blasphemed God because of the plague of the hail; for the plague thereof was exceeding great. And there came one of the seven angels which had the seven vials, and talked with me, saying unto me, Come hither; I will shew unto thee the judgment of the great whore that sitteth upon many waters: With whom the kings of the earth have committed fornication, and the inhabitants of the earth have been made drunk with the wine of her fornication. So he carried me away in the spirit into the wilderness: and I saw a woman sit upon a scarlet coloured beast, full of names of blasphemy, having seven heads and ten horns. And the woman was arrayed in purple and scarlet colour, and decked with gold and precious stones and pearls, having a golden cup in her hand full of abominations and filthiness of her fornication: And upon her forehead was a name written, MYSTERY, BABYLON THE GREAT, THE MOTHER OF HARLOTS AND ABOMINATIONS OF THE EARTH. And I saw the woman drunken with the blood of the saints, and with the blood of the martyrs of Jesus: and when I saw her, I wondered with great admiration. And the angel said unto me, Wherefore didst thou marvel? I will tell thee the mystery of the woman, and of the beast that carrieth her, which hath the seven heads and ten horns. The beast that thou sawest was, and is not; and shall ascend out of the bottomless pit, and go into perdition: and they that dwell on the earth shall wonder, whose names were not written in the book of life from the foundation of the world, when they behold the beast that was, and is not, and yet is. And here is the mind which hath wisdom. The seven heads are seven mountains, on which the woman sitteth. And there are seven kings: five are fallen, and one is, and the other is not yet come; and when he cometh, he must continue a short space. And the beast that was, and is not, even he is the eighth, and is of the seven, and goeth into perdition. And the ten horns which thou sawest are ten kings, which have received no kingdom as yet; but receive power as kings one hour with the beast. These have one mind, and shall give their power and strength unto the beast. These shall make war with the Lamb, and the Lamb shall overcome them: for he is Lord of lords, and King of kings: and they that are with him are called, and chosen, and faithful. And he saith unto me, The waters which thou sawest, where the whore sitteth, are peoples, and multitudes, and nations, and tongues. And the ten horns which thou sawest upon the beast, these shall hate the whore, and shall make her desolate and naked, and shall eat her flesh, and burn her with fire. For God hath put in their hearts to fulfil his will, and to agree, and give their kingdom unto the beast, until the words of God shall be fulfilled. And the woman which thou sawest is that great city, which reigneth over the kings of the earth.

—REVELATION 16:8–17:18

And after these things I saw another angel come down from heaven, having great power; and the earth was lightened with his glory. And he cried mightily with a strong voice, saying, Babylon the great is fallen, is fallen, and is become the habitation of devils, and the hold of every foul spirit, and a cage of every unclean and hateful bird. For all nations have drunk of the wine of the wrath of her fornication, and the kings of the earth have committed fornication with her, and the merchants of the earth are waxed rich through the abundance of her delicacies. And I heard another voice from heaven, saying, Come out of her, my people, that ye be not partakers of her sins, and that ye receive not of her plagues. For her sins have reached unto heaven, and God hath remembered her iniquities. Reward her even as she rewarded you, and double unto her double according to her works: in the cup which she hath filled fill to her double. How much she hath glorified herself, and lived deliciously, so much torment and sorrow give her: for she saith in her heart, I sit a queen, and am no widow, and shall see no sorrow. Therefore shall her plagues come in one day, death, and mourning, and famine; and she shall be utterly burned with fire: for strong is the Lord God who judgeth her. And the kings of the earth, who have committed fornication and lived deliciously with her, shall bewail her, and lament for her, when they shall see the smoke of her burning, Standing afar off for the fear of her torment, saying, Alas, alas that great city Babylon, that mighty city! for in one hour is thy judgment come. And the merchants of the earth shall weep and mourn over her; for no man buyeth their merchandise any more: The merchandise of gold, and silver, and precious stones, and of pearls, and fine linen, and purple, and silk, and scarlet, and all thyine wood, and all manner vessels of ivory, and all manner vessels of most precious wood, and of brass, and iron, and marble.

—REVELATION 18:1–12

See Egypt/Pharaoh/Herod for signs, symptoms and manifestations.

# Spirits of Behemoth and Leviathan

THE BOOK OF Job graphically depicts the spiritual powers and strength of these principalities as unconquerable by human ingenuity. I caution readers to ensure that they are fighting within their measure of rule, and fighting under divine cover. Do not go head-to-head with this principality. Allow spiritual *generals* to initiate and orchestrate prayer and spiritual warfare activities concerning these spirits. Remember to pray under divine covering!

Behold now behemoth, which I made with thee; he eateth grass as an ox. Lo now, his strength is in his loins, and his force is in the navel of his belly. He moveth his tail like a cedar: the sinews of his stones are wrapped together. His bones are as strong pieces of brass; his bones are like bars of iron. He is the chief of the ways of God: he that made him can make his sword to approach unto him. Surely the mountains bring him forth food, where all the beasts of the field play. He lieth under the shady trees, in the covert of the reed, and fens. The shady trees cover him with their shadow; the willows of the brook compass him about. Behold, he drinketh up a river, and hasteth not: he trusteth that he can draw up Jordan into his mouth. He taketh it with his eyes: his nose pierceth through snares.

—JOB 40:15–24

Behemoth has a dinosaur or a large, monstrous spirit, oppressive, powerful, hippopotamus-like creature, known for its supernatural strength. It affects:

- Ideologies, geographical, monetary, political/ military strength

- Religious/cultural strongholds

- Witchcraft (control)

- May take you years to dismantle/destroy (communication)

- Becomes violent when attacked

We must implore *Jehovah Gibbor* to divinely cause their:

- Sinews ripped
- Bones crushed

Leviathan is a crocodile-like sea serpent. It is symbolic of Satan (see Revelation 12) and is unconquerable by human strength or carnal weapons:

Canst thou draw out leviathan with an hook? or his tongue with a cord which thou lettest down? Canst thou put an hook into his nose? or bore his jaw through with a thorn? Will he make many supplications unto thee? will he speak soft words unto thee? Will he make a covenant with thee? wilt thou take him for a servant for ever? Wilt thou play with him as with a bird? or wilt thou bind him for thy maidens? Shall the companions make a banquet of him? shall they part him among the merchants? Canst thou fill his skin with barbed irons? or his head with fish spears? Lay thine hand upon him, remember the battle, do no more. Behold, the hope of him is in vain: shall not one be cast down even at the sight of him? None is so fierce that dare stir him up: who then is able to stand before me? Who hath prevented me, that I should repay him? whatsoever is under the whole heaven is mine. I will not conceal his parts, nor his power, nor his comely proportion. Who can discover the face of his garment? or who can come to him with his double bridle? Who can open the doors of his face? his teeth are terrible round about. His scales are his pride, shut up together as with a close seal. One is so near to another, that no air can come between them. They are joined one to another, they stick together, that they cannot be sundered. By his neesings a light doth shine, and his eyes are like the eyelids of the morning. Out of his mouth go burning lamps, and sparks of fire leap out. Out of his nostrils goeth smoke, as out of a seething pot or caldron. His breath kindleth coals, and a flame goeth out of his mouth. In his neck remaineth strength, and sorrow is turned into joy before him. The flakes of his flesh are joined together: they are firm in themselves; they cannot be moved. His heart is as firm as a stone; yea, as hard as a piece of the nether millstone.

When he raiseth up himself, the mighty are afraid: by reason of breakings they purify themselves. The sword of him that layeth at him cannot hold: the spear, the dart, nor the habergeon. He esteemeth iron as straw, and brass as rotten wood. The arrow cannot make him flee: slingstones are turned with him into stubble. Darts are counted as stubble: he laugheth at the shaking of a spear. Sharp stones are under him: he spreadeth sharp pointed things upon the mire. He maketh the deep to boil like a pot: he maketh the sea like a pot of ointment. He maketh a path to shine after him; one would think the deep to be hoary. Upon earth there is not his like, who is made without fear. He beholdeth all high things: he is a king over all the children of pride.

—JOB 41:1–34

Thou brakest the heads of leviathan in pieces, and gavest him to be meat to the people inhabiting the wilderness.

—PSALM 74:14

There go the ships: there is that leviathan, whom thou hast made to play therein.

—PSALM 104:26

In that day the LORD with his sore and great and strong sword shall punish leviathan the piercing serpent, even leviathan that crooked serpent; and he shall slay the dragon that is in the sea.

—ISAIAH 27:1

See Spirit of Oppression and Spirits of Egypt/Pharaoh/Herod for signs, symptoms and manifestations.

# Mammon

Mammon is the financial and economic system and currency of Babylon. It has a personality and can be made a friend or foe, a master or a slave. The word *mammon* is Chaldean in origin and is translated in English as *wealth*. In the Old Testament, we are told that the wealth (mammon) of the wicked is laid up for the righteous. However, we must be very cautious as we approach this particular spirit, to remember that our priorities must be in order. In pursuing mammon we must first be sold out to God. Matthew 6:24 states, "No man can serve two masters: for either he will hate the one, and love the other; or else he will hold to the one, and despise the other. Ye cannot serve God and mammon." Secondly we must make the pursuit of His Kingdom our priority.

> And I say unto you, Make to yourselves friends of the mammon of unrighteousness; that, when ye fail, they may receive you into everlasting habitations.
> —LUKE 16:9

> If therefore ye have not been faithful in the unrighteous mammon, who will commit to your trust the true riches?
> —LUKE 16:11

> But seek ye first the Kingdom of God, and his righteousness, and all these things shall be added unto you.
> —MATTHEW 6:33

See Spirit of Oppression and Spirits of Egypt/Pharaoh/Herod for signs, symptoms and manifestations.

# Spirit of Balaam

THE SPIRIT OF Balaam is a spirit that causes an individual to compromise his convictions, forfeit ministry, disobey divine directives, and sell his soul for money.

Jude, the servant of Jesus Christ, and brother of James, to them that are sanctified by God the Father, and preserved in Jesus Christ, and called: Mercy unto you, and peace, and love, be multiplied. Beloved, when I gave all diligence to write unto you of the common salvation, it was needful for me to write unto you, and exhort you that ye should earnestly contend for the faith which was once delivered unto the saints. For there are certain men crept in unawares, who were before of old ordained to this condemnation, ungodly men, turning the grace of our God into lasciviousness, and denying the only Lord God, and our Lord Jesus Christ. I will therefore put you in remembrance, though ye once knew this, how that the Lord, having saved the people out of the land of Egypt, afterward destroyed them that believed not. And the angels which kept not their first estate, but left their own habitation, he hath reserved in everlasting chains under darkness unto the judgment of the great day. Even as Sodom and Gomorrha, and the cities about them in like manner, giving themselves over to fornication, and going after strange flesh, are set forth for an example, suffering the vengeance of eternal fire. Likewise also these filthy dreamers defile the flesh, despise dominion, and speak evil of dignities. Yet Michael the archangel, when contending with the devil he disputed about the body of Moses, durst not bring against him a railing accusation, but said, The Lord rebuke thee. But these speak evil of those things which they know not: but what they know naturally, as brute beasts, in those things they corrupt themselves. Woe unto them! for they have gone in the way of Cain, and ran greedily after the error of Balaam for reward, and perished in the gainsaying of Core. These are spots in your feasts of charity, when they feast with you, feeding themselves without fear: clouds they are without water, carried about of winds; trees whose fruit withereth, without fruit, twice dead, plucked up by the roots; Raging waves of the sea, foaming out their own shame; wandering stars, to whom is reserved the blackness of darkness for ever. And Enoch also, the seventh from Adam, prophesied of these, saying, Behold, the Lord cometh with ten thousands of his saints, To execute judgment upon all, and to convince all that are ungodly among them of all their ungodly deeds which they have ungodly committed, and of all their hard speeches which ungodly sinners have spoken against him. These are murmurers, complainers, walking after their own lusts; and their mouth speaketh great swelling words, having men's persons in admiration because of advantage. But, beloved, remember ye the words which were spoken before of the apostles of our Lord Jesus Christ; How that they told you there should be mockers in the last time, who should walk after their own ungodly lusts. These be they who separate themselves, sensual, having not the Spirit.

—JUDE 1–19

But there were false prophets also among the people, even as there shall be false teachers among you, who privily shall bring in damnable heresies, even denying the Lord that bought them, and bring upon themselves swift destruction. And many shall follow their pernicious ways; by reason of whom the way of truth shall be evil spoken of. And through covetousness shall they with feigned words make merchandise of you: whose judgment now of a long time lingereth not, and their damnation slumbereth not. For if God spared not the angels that sinned, but cast them down to hell, and delivered them into chains of darkness, to be reserved unto judgment; And spared not the old world, but saved Noah the eighth person, a preacher of righteousness, bringing in the flood upon the world of the ungodly; And turning the cities of Sodom and Gomorrha into ashes condemned them with an overthrow, making them an ensample unto those that after should live ungodly; And delivered just Lot, vexed with the filthy conversation of the wicked: (For that righteous man dwelling among them, in seeing and hearing, vexed his righteous soul from day to day with their unlawful deeds); The Lord knoweth how to deliver the godly out of temptations, and to reserve the unjust unto the day of judgment to be punished: But chiefly them that walk after the flesh in the lust of uncleanness, and despise government. Presumptuous are they, self-willed, they are not afraid to speak evil of dignities. Whereas angels, which are greater in power and might, bring not railing accusation against them before the Lord. But these, as natural brute beasts, made to be taken and destroyed, speak evil of the things that they understand not; and shall utterly perish in their own corruption; And shall receive the reward of unrighteousness, as they that count it pleasure to riot in the day time. Spots they are and blemishes, sporting themselves with their own deceivings while they feast with you; Having eyes full of adultery, and that cannot cease from sin; beguiling unstable souls: an heart they have exercised with covetous practices; cursed children: Which have forsaken the right way, and are gone astray, following the way of Balaam the son of Bosor, who loved the wages of unrighteousness; But was rebuked for his iniquity: the dumb ass speaking with man's voice forbad the madness of the prophet. These are wells without water, clouds that are carried with a tempest; to whom the mist of darkness is reserved for ever. For when they speak great swelling words of vanity, they allure through the lusts of the flesh, through much wantonness, those that were clean escaped from them who live in error. While they promise them liberty, they themselves are the servants of corruption: for of whom a man is overcome, of the same is he brought in bondage. For if after they have escaped the pollutions of the world through the knowledge of the Lord and Saviour Jesus Christ, they are again entangled therein, and overcome, the latter end is worse with them than the beginning. For it had been better for them not to have known the way of righteousness, than, after they have known it, to turn from the holy commandment delivered unto them. But it is happened unto them according to the true proverb, The dog is turned to his own vomit again; and the sow that was washed to her wallowing in the mire.

—2 PETER 2:1–22

Let no man say when he is tempted, I am tempted of God: for God cannot be tempted with evil, neither tempteth he any man: But every man is tempted, when he is drawn away of his own lust, and enticed. Then when lust hath conceived, it bringeth forth sin: and sin, when it is finished, bringeth forth death. Do not err, my beloved brethren.

—JAMES 1:13–16

But I have a few things against thee, because thou hast there them that hold the doctrine of Balaam, who taught Balac to cast a stumbling block before the children of Israel, to eat things sacrificed unto idols, and to commit fornication.

—REVELATION 2:14

| Signs, Symptoms, and Manifestations of the Spirit of Balaam | | |
|---|---|---|
| Greed | Filthy lucre | Compromise |
| Temptation | Iniquity | Sin |
| Lust | Selfishness | Self-centeredness |
| Contaminated anointing | Betrayal | Carnality |
| Perversion | Misrepresentation | Worldliness |
| Fraud | | |

**Release:** Purity of heart, consecrated life, integrity, honesty.

# Spirit of Belial

THIS OUTLAW SPIRIT works in confederation with the spirit of Jezebel. It is a spirit assigned to destroy influence, sabotage ministries, undermine authority, and pilfer property. I call this spirit the spiritual mob because of its gangster-like characteristics.

> Certain men, the children of Belial, are gone out from among you, and have withdrawn the inhabitants of their city, saying, Let us go and serve other gods, which ye have not known.
>
> —DEUTERONOMY 13:13

Now as they were making their hearts merry, behold, the men of the city, certain sons of Belial, beset the house round about, and beat at the door, and spake to the master of the house, the old man, saying, Bring forth the man that came into thine house, that we may know him. And the man, the master of the house, went out unto them, and said unto them, Nay, my brethren, nay, I pray you, do not so wickedly; seeing that this man is come into mine house, do not this folly.

—JUDGES 19:22–23

Count not thine handmaid for a daughter of Belial: for out of the abundance of my complaint and grief have I spoken hitherto.

—1 SAMUEL 1:16

Now the sons of Eli were sons of Belial; they knew not the LORD.

—1 SAMUEL 2:12

But the children of Belial said, How shall this man save us? And they despised him, and brought him no presents. But he held his peace.

—1 SAMUEL 10:27

Now therefore know and consider what thou wilt do; for evil is determined against our master, and against all his household: for he is such a son of Belial, that a man cannot speak to him.

—1 SAMUEL 25:17

Then answered all the wicked men and men of Belial, of those that went with David, and said, Because they went not with us, we will not give them ought of the spoil that we have recovered, save to every man his wife and his children, that they may lead them away, and depart.

—1 SAMUEL 30:22

And set two men, sons of Belial, before him, to bear witness against him, saying, Thou didst blaspheme God and the king. And then carry him out, and stone him, that he may die. And the men of his city, even the elders and the nobles who were the inhabitants in his city, did as Jezebel had sent unto them, and as it was written in the letters which she had sent unto them. They proclaimed a fast, and set Naboth on high among the people. And there came in two men, children of Belial, and sat before him: and the men of Belial witnessed against him, even against Naboth, in the presence of the people, saying, Naboth did blaspheme God and the king. Then they carried him forth out of the city, and stoned him with stones, that he died.

—1 Kings 21:10–13

| Signs, Symptoms, and Manifestations of the Spirit of Belial | | |
|---|---|---|
| Rebellion | Insubordination | Lust |
| Character assassination | Pilfering | Sabotage |
| Treachery | Violence | Perversion |
| Murder | Harassment | Deception |
| Selfishness | Riotous living | Slander |
| Carnality | Sensuality | Falsehood |
| Unrighteousness | False accusation | Works of darkness |
| Witchcraft | Gossip | Lying |
| Maligning character | | |

**Release:** The spirit of Jehu, the fear of the Lord, and boldness.

# Spirit of Carnality

THE WORD *CARNALITY* comes from the Greek word *sarkikos*, which, when translated into English, connotes "rotten" flesh. Anti-spiritual in nature, this spirit appeals to the appetite of the soul. Isaiah 29:8 gives us greater insight, "It shall even be as when an hungry man dreameth, and, behold, he eateth; but he awaketh, and his soul is empty: or as when a thirsty man dreameth, and, behold, he drinketh; but he awaketh, and, behold, he is faint, and his soul hath appetite."

**Lusts:** are evil desires that readily express themselves in bodily activities. They are the "natural" tendency of the flesh and the soulish capacity and proclivity to gravitate toward things that are evil. Some lusts may characteristically be "refined" as in the pride of life, but they are still lusts.

Desire in and of itself is not to be feared. God promises us the desires of our hearts in Psalm 37:4. Lust, however, is perverted desire that leads to sin. When lust prevails in our lives, we may get what we want, but we will lose what we have.

And the mixt multitude that was among them fell a lusting: and the children of Israel also wept again, and said, Who shall give us flesh to eat? We remember the fish, which we did eat in Egypt freely; the cucumbers, and the melons, and the leeks, and the onions, and the garlick....And there went forth a wind from the Lord, and brought quails from the sea, and let them fall by the camp, as it were a day's journey on this side, and as it were a day's journey on the other side, round about the camp, and as it were two cubits high upon the face of the earth. And the people stood up all that day, and all that night, and all the next day, and they gathered the quails: he that gathered least gathered ten homers: and they spread them all abroad for themselves round about the camp. And while the flesh was yet between their teeth, ere it was chewed, the wrath of the Lord was kindled against the people, and the Lord smote the people with a very great plague.

—Numbers 11:4–5, 31–33

And likewise also the men, leaving the natural use of the woman, burned in their lust one toward another; men with men working that which is unseemly, and receiving in themselves that recompense of their error which was meet.

—Romans 1:27

Let not sin therefore reign in your mortal body, that ye should obey it in the lusts thereof.

—Romans 6:12

O wretched man that I am! who shall deliver me from the body of this death?

—Romans 7:24

For they that are after the flesh do mind the things of the flesh; but they that are after the Spirit the things of the Spirit. For to be carnally minded is death; but to be spiritually minded is life and peace. Because the carnal mind is enmity against God: for it is not subject to the law of God, neither indeed can be. So then they that are in the flesh cannot please God.

—ROMANS 8:5–8

But put ye on the Lord Jesus Christ, and make not provision for the flesh, to fulfil the lusts thereof.

—ROMANS 13:14

This I say then, Walk in the Spirit, and ye shall not fulfil the lust of the flesh. For the flesh lusteth against the Spirit, and the Spirit against the flesh: and these are contrary the one to the other: so that ye cannot do the things that ye would.

—GALATIANS 5:16–17

Now the works of the flesh are manifest, which are these; Adultery, fornication, uncleanness, lasciviousness, Idolatry, witchcraft, hatred, variance, emulations, wrath, strife, seditions, heresies, Envyings, murders, drunkenness, revellings, and such like: of the which I tell you before, as I have also told you in time past, that they which do such things shall not inherit the kingdom of God.

—GALATIANS 5:19–21

Let no corrupt communication proceed out of your mouth, but that which is good to the use of edifying, that it may minister grace unto the hearers....For this ye know, that no whoremonger, nor unclean person, nor covetous man, who is an idolater, hath any inheritance in the kingdom of Christ and of God.

—EPHESIANS 4:29; 5:5

Let no man say when he is tempted, I am tempted of God: for God cannot be tempted with evil, neither tempteth he any man: But every man is tempted, when he is drawn away of his own lust, and enticed. Then when lust hath conceived, it bringeth forth sin: and sin, when it is finished, bringeth forth death. Do not err, my beloved brethren.... From whence come wars and fightings among you? come they not hence, even of your lusts that war in your members? Ye lust, and have not: ye kill, and desire to have, and cannot obtain: ye fight and war, yet ye have not, because ye ask not. Ye ask, and receive not, because ye ask amiss, that ye may consume it upon your lusts. Ye adulterers and adulteresses, know ye not that the friendship of the world is enmity with God? whosoever therefore will be a friend of the world is the enemy of God. Do ye think that the scripture saith in vain, The spirit that dwelleth in us lusteth to envy? But he giveth more grace. Wherefore he saith, God resisteth the proud, but giveth grace unto the humble.

—JAMES 1:13–16; 4:1–6

## Fruit of the Spirit

But the fruit of the Spirit is love, joy, peace, long-suffering, gentleness, goodness, faith, Meekness, temperance: against such there is no law.

—GALATIANS 5:22–23

## Manifestation of the Spirit

But the manifestation of the Spirit is given to every man to profit withal. For to one is given by the Spirit the word of wisdom; to another the word of knowledge by the same Spirit; to another faith by the same Spirit; to another the gifts of healing by the same Spirit; To another the working of miracles; to another prophecy; to another discerning of spirits; to another divers kinds of tongues; to another the interpretation of tongues.

—1 Corinthians 12:7–10

| Signs, Symptoms, and Manifestations of Lusts of the Flesh | | |
|---|---|---|
| Adultery | Fornication | Clamor |
| Uncleanness | Lasciviousness | Rage |
| Idolatry | Witchcraft | Malice |
| Hatred | Variance | Slander |
| Emulations | Wrath | Filthy language |
| Strife | Seditions | Lying |
| False witness | Ingratitude | Complaining |
| Heresies | Envy | Deception |
| Sexual sins[1] | Gambling | Railing |
| Temptations | Seduction (enticing) | Error |
| Judgmentalism | Presumptuous living | Reviling |
| Immorality | Fighting | Killing |

[1]Sexual sin sanctification eliminates and displaces sensuality. It has three stages: initial, progressive, and final.

| Dissatisfaction | Evil thoughts | Selfishness |
| --- | --- | --- |
| Worldliness | Pride | Unrighteousness |
| Rebellion | Anarchy | Iniquities of the heart |
| Greed | Comparing | Hoarding |
| Compromises | Grumbling | Anger |
| Doubt | Bitterness | Covetousness |
| Ungratefulness | Arrogance | "Worldliness" |
| Evil desires | Plagues/ diseases | Faulty perspectives |
| Death | Ill will | Spite |
| Murders | Drunkenness | Brawling |
| Revelings | Resentment | Addictions (of all kinds) |
| Lusts (of all kinds) | Animosity | Perversion (see listing) |
| Fault-finding | Gluttony | Quarreling |
| Effeminacy | Alcoholism | Dissatisfaction with God's provisions |
| Abusive/ blasphemous language | | |

## Lust of the Eye

But I say unto you, That whosoever looketh on a woman to lust after her hath committed adultery with her already in his heart.

—Matthew 5:28

What shall we say then? Is the law sin? God forbid. Nay, I had not known sin, but by the law: for I had not known lust, except the law had said, Thou shalt not covet.

—ROMANS 7:7

Now these things were our examples, to the intent we should not lust after evil things, as they also lusted. Neither be ye idolaters, as were some of them; as it is written, The people sat down to eat and drink, and rose up to play. Neither let us commit fornication, as some of them committed, and fell in one day three and twenty thousand. Neither let us tempt Christ, as some of them also tempted, and were destroyed of serpents. Neither murmur ye, as some of them also murmured, and were destroyed of the destroyer.

—1 CORINTHIANS 10:6–10

| Signs, Symptoms, and Manifestations of Lust of the Eye | | |
|---|---|---|
| Greed | Covetousness | Gluttony |
| Stealing | Cruelty | Extortion |
| Kleptomania | Abandonment | Perversion |
| Discontentment | Envy | |

## Pride of Life

For all that is in the world, the lust of the flesh, and the lust of the eyes, and the pride of life, is not of the Father, but is of the world.

—1 JOHN 2:16

Let no man beguile you of your reward in a voluntary humility and worshipping of angels, intruding into those things which he hath not seen, vainly puffed up by his fleshly mind.

—COLOSSIANS 2:18

| Signs, Symptoms, and Manifestations of the Pride of Life | | |
|---|---|---|
| Flamboyance | Pride of possession | Stubbornness |
| Grandiosity | Inordinate sophistication | Vain glory |
| Superiority | Narcissism | Formalism |
| Religiosity | Arrogance | Historical/cultural/generational pride |

**Release**: Deliverance, holiness, fruit of the Spirit, and manifestations of the Spirit.

# Spirit of Competition

THIS SPIRIT CREATES rivalry between entities, who compete for the same prize or profit. This spirit is slick and covertly fulfills its mission. Competition is a door-keeping spirit. It opens doors to other stronger and more deadly spirits:

> And I commanded, and search hath been made, and it is found that this city of old time hath made insurrection against kings, and that rebellion and sedition have been made therein.
>
> —EZRA 4:19

> Therefore said some of the Pharisees, This man is not of God, because he keepeth not the sabbath day. Others said, How can a man that is a sinner do such miracles? And there was a division among them....There was a division therefore again among the Jews for these sayings.
>
> —JOHN 9:16; 10:19

## Signs, Symptoms, and Manifestations of the Spirit of Competition

| | | |
|---|---|---|
| Isolation | Resentment | Alienation |
| Retaliation | Strife | Discord |
| Broken relationships | Emulation | Spite |
| Sedition | Game playing | Accusations |
| Rivalry | Slander | Opposition |
| Gossip | Contention | Contempt |
| Wrath | Heresy | Hypocrisy |
| Deceit | Stigmatization | Territorialism |
| Withholding | Disharmony | Jealousy |
| Underhandedness | Antagonism | Detachment |
| Divorce | Rebellions | Defiance |
| Ill will | Unfair practices | |

**Release:** Fellowship, unity, love, forgiveness, harmony, compliance, obedience, and discernment.

# The Spirit of Confusion

THE SPIRIT OF confusion causes disorder and disarray in the life and relationships of many people. It also causes an individual to live in a stunned and cluttered condition, confusing the mind, bewildering the emotions and distressing relationships. This spirit works with the spirit of madness.

> For God is not the author of confusion, but of peace, as in all churches of the saints.
>
> —1 CORINTHIANS 14:33

> For where envying and strife is, there is confusion and every evil work.
>
> —JAMES 3:16

| Signs, Symptoms, and Manifestations of the Spirit of Confusion | | |
|---|---|---|
| Defensiveness | Argumentative | Attitudes |
| Loss of memory | Preoccupation | Lack of direction |

| Lack of purpose | Lack of goals | Envy |
|---|---|---|
| Trance-like states | Strife | Shame |
| Hypnotic (stupor) state | Covetousness | Spite |
| Aimlessness | Clutter | Disorganization |
| Disarray | Disorder | Bewilderment |
| Self-conscious distress | Distraction | Strife |
| Emotional disturbance | Pandemonium | Furor |
| Bedlam | Discomposure | Bafflement |
| Befuddlement | Fretting | Uproar |
| Tumult | Turmoil | Discomfiture |
| Fluster | Upsets | Embarrassment |
| Perplexity | Nervousness | Humiliation |
| Perturbation | Double-mindedness | Awkwardness |
| Feelings of discontentment and resentment | Loss of mental acuity/discernment/ acumen/perception/ sharpness | |

**Release:** The mind of Christ, God's original plan and purpose, and peace, love, and soundness of mind and order.

# Deaf and Dumb Spirit

ALTHOUGH THIS SPIRIT is seen through many countries and communities, this spirit is often assigned to children and spouses of leadership. It acts as both a door and gatekeeper for other spirits, and distracts the man or woman of God from fulfilling their assignment. The deaf and dumb spirit is known to target children, attaching itself to a baby while yet in the womb.

> When Jesus saw that the people came running together, he rebuked the foul spirit, saying unto him, Thou dumb and deaf spirit, I charge thee, come out of him, and enter no more into him.
>
> —MARK 9:25

| Signs, Symptoms, and Manifestations of the Deaf and Dumb Spirit | | |
|---|---|---|
| Drug and alcohol abuse | Childish self-will | Suicidal thoughts |
| Daydreaming | Seizures | Convulsions |

| Depression | Repression | Inability to speak |
|---|---|---|
| Deafness (natural/spiritual) | Speech impediments | Extreme immaturity |
| Tremors | Addictions | Ticks |
| Mental/ psychological disorders | Attention deficit disorders | Physiological/ emotional dysfunctions |
| Sleepiness (especially during the preaching of the Word of God) | | |

**Release:** Deliverance, liberty, life, divine health and healing.

# Spirit of Death

THIS SPIRIT IS assigned to terminate and cause entities to become extinct. There are many kinds of death you can experience. They are:

- Physical death

- Emotional death, which shuts the emotions down and makes you emotionally numb, indifferent, or nonfeeling

- Spiritual death, which can come in the form of reprobation here on Earth, or eternal separation from God in the afterlife

- Relational death, such as divorce

- Social death, such as the loss of influence or reputation, life-imprisonment

- Financial death, which can be caused by failure to perceive opportunities, or the misappropriation of funds.

I will ransom them from the power of the grave; I

will redeem them from death: O death, I will be thy plagues; O grave, I will be thy destruction: repentance shall be hid from mine eyes.

—HOSEA 13:14

The sorrows of hell compassed me about: the snares of death prevented me.

—PSALM 18:5

Let death seize upon them, and let them go down quick into hell: for wickedness is in their dwellings, and among them.

—PSALM 55:15

For great is thy mercy toward me: and thou hast delivered my soul from the lowest hell.

—PSALM 86:13

The sorrows of death compassed me, and the pains of hell gat hold upon me: I found trouble and sorrow.

—PSALM 116:3

For the wages of sin is death; but the gift of God is eternal life through Jesus Christ our Lord.

—ROMANS 6:23

| Signs, Symptoms, and Manifestations of the Spirit of Death | | |
|---|---|---|
| Murder | Suicide | Homicide |
| Miscarriage | Abortion | Divorce |
| Morbidity | Grief | Despondency |
| Depression | Hopelessness | Oppression |
| Gossip | Slander | Jealousy |

| Fratricide | Railing[1] | Stigmatization |
| --- | --- | --- |
| Character assassination | Imprisonment | Discouragement |
| Disillusionment | Betrayal | Isolation |
| Emotional wounds | Sorrow | Loss |
| Wages of sin | Ill-spoken words | Indifference |
| Maligning of character | Unbelief | Terminal illnesses |
| Spiritual blindness | Homosexuality | Lost opportunities |
| Untimely death | Accidents | Loss of hope |
| Loss of vision | Deprivation | Disease |
|  |  |  |

**Release:** Divine healing, health, life, and reversal of the death cycle.

---

[1]Railing: verbal insults, to utter reproach; to charge with a fault in language; cutting expressions of blame, disgrace, contempt, or derision.

# Spirit of Depression

DEPRESSION IS A mental disease that plagues every society. Psychologically speaking, depression is a psychotic or neurotic condition characterized by inability, feelings of heaviness and melancholy, extreme sadness, hopelessness, and often insomnia.

| Signs, Symptoms, and Manifestations of the Spirit of Depression | | |
|---|---|---|
| Sadness | Melancholy | Despondency |
| Memory loss | Crying spells | Loss of energy |
| Chronic fatigue | Loss of appetite | Loss of focus |
| Increase in appetite | Desperation | Hopelessness |
| Distractions | Preoccupations | Lack of focus |
| Nonchalant attitude | Suicidal tendency | Frustration |
| Feelings of alienation | Homicidal tendency | Gloominess |

| "Staring into space" | Need for approval | Unhappiness |
|---|---|---|
| Despair | Dejection | Listlessness |
| Drab/darkness of mind | Need assistance | Sleepiness |
| Excessive sleeping | Confusion | Insomnia |
| Anxiety | Strong external locus of control | Feelings of loneliness and aloneness |
| Irregular sleeping patterns/habits | Dependent personality (need assistance to achieve "normal" things) | |

**Release:** The anointing, peace, the mind of Christ, and joy.

# Spirit of Desolation

THIS SPIRIT CAUSES loss, abandonment, a state of anguish, and deprivation. Desolation can be manifested as a natural phenomenon, emotional, physical, social, or psychological condition. This spirit causes loss, abandonment, a state of anguish, deprival, barrenness, and the lack of prosperity.

> So that the LORD could no longer bear, because of the evil of your doings, and because of the abominations which ye have committed; therefore is your land a desolation, and an astonishment, and a curse, without an inhabitant, as at this day.
>
> —JEREMIAH 44:22

> And Jesus knew their thoughts, and said unto them, Every kingdom divided against itself is brought to desolation; and every city or house divided against itself shall not stand.
>
> —MATTHEW 12:25

## Signs, Symptoms, and Manifestations of the Spirit of Desolation

| | | |
|---|---|---|
| Immorality | Religion | Subversion |
| Accusation | Suspicion | Poverty |
| Idolatry | Unrighteousness | Unrighteous mammon |
| Hardship | Oppression | Greed |
| Vexation | Sedition | Jealousy |
| Pharisee/ Sadducee spirit | Spiritual dryness | Morbidity |
| Depression | Spiritual darkness | Spiritual bondage |
| Hopelessness | Murder | |

**Release**: Meekness, moderation, purity of heart, a spirit of vengeance, holiness, true and pure worship.

# Spirit of Divination

THIS SPIRIT IS often one of the spirits responsible for blatant anarchy of the pew and rebellion of parishioners. The spirit of rebellion is the foundation upon which Satan and the kingdom of darkness is built. The divination principality often attempts to counterfeit the work of the Holy Spirit. Rebellion is to divination as the anointing is to the Holy Spirit.

> There shall not be found among you any one that maketh his son or daughter to pass through the fire, or that useth divination, or an observer of times, or an enchanter, or a witch, Or a charmer, or a consulter with familiar spirits, or a wizard, or a necromancer. For all that do these things are an abomination unto the LORD: and because of these abominations the LORD thy God doth drive them out from before thee.
>
> —DEUTERONOMY 18:10–12

And it came to pass, as we went to prayer, a certain damsel possessed with a spirit of divination met us, which brought her masters much gain by soothsaying.

—ACTS 16:16

## Signs, Symptoms, and Manifestations of the Spirit of Divination

| | | |
|---|---|---|
| Controlling spirit | Mind control | Psychic activities |
| Palm reading | Obeah | Voodoo |
| Horoscope | Drugs | Incantations |
| Cultic activities/rituals | Witchcraft | Occult |
| White magic | Black magic | Conjuration |
| Charms | Prognostication | Railing |
| Wizardry | Hypnosis | Hexes |
| Omens | Idolatry | Fortune telling |
| Necromancy | Astral projection | Sorcery/ soothsaying |
| Unrighteous mammon | Vexation/grief | Superstition |
| False prophets | Ill-spoken | Words/wishes/ malice |
| Familiar spirits | False prophets | Enchanters |
| Dreamers | Diviners | Water-watchers |
| Tea leaf readers | Rebellion | Blasphemy |
| Automatic writings | Ouija Board | Masonry |
| Illumination | Oppression | Spirit of Belial |

| Antagonism | Coercion | Aanarchy fear |
|---|---|---|
| Dreams | Strange occurrences | Control |
| Violence | Illuminati | Irritations |
| Stirrings | Frustrations | Temptations |
| Harassments | Accusations | Irritations |
| Perversions | Impressions | Concentrations |
| Interceptions | Provocations | Negotiations |
| Contentions | Prohibitions | Deceptions |
| Inhibitions | Alterations | Persecutions |
| Character assassinations | Suicide | Murder |
| Subversions | Insinuations | Illusions |
| Disillusions | Projections | Suspicions |
| Manipulations | Deprivation | Desolation |
| Demonic activities | Depression | Misrepresentations |
| Justifications | Rationalizations | Misinformation |
| Afflictions | Addictions | Dysfunctions |
| Speculations | Stigmas | Satanic operations |
| Decisions | Conclusions | Distortions |
| Seduction | Attractions | Divination |
| Astrology | Misfortunes | Mishaps |
| Associations | Relations | Resolutions |
| Fantasies | Assaults | Alliances |
| Insults | Impure motives | Irritations |
| Bands | Slanders | Burdens |
| Discouragements | Confusion | Divisions |
| Interference | Snares | Entanglements |

| Misunderstandings | Denial | Rulings |
|---|---|---|
| Resistance | Diseases | Ailments |
| Defects | Disabilities | Disorders |
| Infections | Infirmities | Victimization |
| Connections | Contaminations | Alcoholism |
| Unexplainable accidents | Inordinate affections | Neurotic and psychotic behaviors and tendencies |
| Attachments (include the use of talisman, books, clothing, furniture, jewelry, etc.) | | |

**Release:** The anointing, the manifestation of the gifts of the Spirit, prophetic anointing, apostolic anointing, anointing of Elijah, anointing of Jehu.

# Spirits of Egypt, Pharaoh, and Herod

THE SPIRIT OF Egypt is a spirit that oppresses groupings of people at a national or global level. On the one hand, these spirits utilize the body and souls of man to further their economic and spiritual cause, and, on the other hand, they are responsible for abortion and assassination. The greatest atrocity is not that of becoming a physical prisoner of war, but a psychological prisoner of war.

And the children of Israel were fruitful, and increased abundantly, and multiplied, and waxed exceeding mighty; and the land was filled with them. Now there arose up a new king over Egypt, which knew not Joseph. And he said unto his people, Behold, the people of the children of Israel are more and mightier than we: Come on, let us deal wisely with them; lest they multiply, and it come to pass, that, when there falleth out any war, they join also unto our enemies, and fight against us, and so get them up out of the land. Therefore they did set over them taskmasters to afflict them with their burdens. And they built for Pharaoh treasure cities, Pithom and Raamses. But the more they afflicted them, the more they multiplied and grew. And they were grieved because of the children of Israel. And the Egyptians made the children of Israel to serve with rigour: And they made their lives bitter with hard bondage, in morter, and in brick, and in all manner of service in the field: all their service, wherein they made them serve, was with rigour. And the king of Egypt spake to the Hebrew midwives, of which the name of the one was Shiphrah, and the name of the other Puah: And he said, When ye do the office of a midwife to the Hebrew women, and see them upon the stools; if it be a son, then ye shall kill him: but if it be a daughter, then she shall live. But the midwives feared God, and did not as the king of Egypt commanded them, but saved the men children alive. And the king of Egypt called for the midwives, and said unto them, Why have ye done this thing, and have saved the men children alive? And the midwives said unto Pharaoh, Because the Hebrew women are not as the Egyptian women; for they are lively, and are delivered ere the midwives come in unto them. Therefore God dealt well with the midwives: and the people multiplied, and waxed very mighty. And it came to pass, because the midwives feared God, that he made them houses. And Pharaoh charged all his people, saying, Every son that is born ye shall cast into the river, and every daughter ye shall save alive.

—EXODUS 1:7–22

And the LORD said, I have surely seen the affliction of my people which are in Egypt, and have heard their cry by reason of their taskmasters; for I know their sorrows.

—EXODUS 3:7

Then Herod, when he saw that he was mocked of the wise men, was exceeding wroth, and sent forth, and slew all the children that were in Bethlehem, and in all the coasts thereof, from two years old and under, according to the time which he had diligently inquired of the wise men.

—MATTHEW 2:16

# Types of Slavery Today

**Bonded labour** affects at least twenty million[1] people around the world. People become bonded laborers by taking or being tricked into taking a loan for as little as the cost of medicine for a sick child. To repay the debt, many are forced to work long hours, seven days a week, up to 365 days a year. They receive basic food and shelter as "payment" for their work, but may never pay off the loan, which can be passed down for generations.

**Early and forced marriage** affects women and girls who are married without choice and are forced into lives of servitude often accompanied by physical violence.

**Forced labour** affects people who are illegally recruited by individuals, governments or political parties and forced to work—usually under threat of violence or other penalties.

**Slavery by descent** is where people are either born into a slave class or are from a 'group' that society views as suited to being used as slave labour.

**Trafficking** involves the transport or trade of people—women, children, and men—from one area to another for the purpose of forcing them into slavery conditions.

**Child labour** affects an estimated 179 million[11] children around the world in work that is harmful to their health and welfare.

- Emotional slavery
- Psychological slavery
- Institutionalized religion
- Institutionalized slavery
- Oppression

The individuals controlled by this spirit would have to learn:

- Compassion
- To live as a free person
- Problem-solving skills
- Social skills
- Decision-making skills
- Critical thinking skills
- Values clarification
- How to budget
- Planning and goal setting

| Signs Symptoms and Manifestations of the Spirits of Egypt, Pharaoh, and Herod | | |
|---|---|---|
| Abortion | Abuse | Addictions |
| Affinities | Afflictions | Ailments |

[11]See the "Spirit of Oppression" for further insight.

| Alcoholism | Alienation | Alienation from the life of God |
|---|---|---|
| Alliances | Animalization | Antagonism |
| Antichrist | Antichrist Activities | Anti-Semitism |
| Apartheid | Apathy | Arrogance |
| Assaults | Associations | Atheism |
| Attachments | Attractions | Backlash |
| Backsliding | Bands | Berating |
| Besetting Sin | Betrayal | Black sheep syndrome |
| Blasphemy | Blind trust | Bondage |
| Brutalization | Burdens | Carnality |
| Castigation | Castration | Censorship |
| Chattel slavery | Chemical abuse | Child abuse |
| Class distinction | Codependency | Coercion |
| Communism | Comparison | Competition |
| Confusion | Connections | Conspiracy |
| Consumerism | Contaminations | Contempt |
| Contracts | Corruption | Covenants |
| Criminal activities | Criticism | Crookedness |
| Cross-breeding | Crucifixion | Cruelty |
| Cultural entrenchment | Cultural erosion | Cultural hypnotism |
| Death | Debauchery | Defiance |
| Dehumanization | De-masculinization | Denial |
| Dependence | Depression | Deprivation |
| Desertion | Desolation | Destruction |

| | | |
|---|---|---|
| Devaluation | Dictatorship | Disabilities |
| Disapproval | Discouragement | Discrimination |
| Disdain | Disease | Disempowerment |
| Disenfranchisement | Disharmony | Disillusionment |
| Distrust | Disunity | Divide and conquer |
| Divination | Divisions | Doctrines of devils |
| Doctrines of man | Dominance | Dread |
| Drug addiction | Economic hardship | Economic impotence |
| Economic oppression | Ego-gratification | Embarrassment |
| Emotional conditioning | Emotional deprivation | Emotional slavery |
| Entanglements | Envy | Error |
| Escapism | Family pride | Family secrets |
| Fantasies | Fear | Terror |
| Defects | Filthy lucre | Forced labor |
| Frustration | Genetic manipulation | Genocide |
| Glass ceilings | Grandiosity | Greed |
| Grief | Gross darkness | Guile |
| Habits | Hangings | Harassment |
| Hard-heartedness | Hardship | Harshness |
| Hatred | Helplessness | Herodism |
| High things | Hitlerism | Hopelessness |
| Humanism | Humiliation | Idolatry |
| Ignominy | Immaturity | Immorality |
| Impaired will | Imprisonment | Impure motives |

| Incarceration | Independent spirit | Indifference |
|---|---|---|
| Indignation | Infections | Infirmities |
| Iniquity | Injustice | Insomnia |
| Institutionalize racism | Insufficiencies | Insults |
| Internal unrest | Intimidation | Irresponsibility |
| Irritations | Interference | Interrelation issues |
| Jealousy | Judgmentalism | Justification |
| Knowledge blocks | Labeling | Learned helplessness |
| Legalism | Legalization | Loss of dignity |
| Lust (all forms) | Lynching | Maiming |
| Manipulation | Maladaptive sets of behavior | Male castigation |
| Malice | Master-slave relations | Materialism |
| Memory loss | Mental affliction | Mental/emotional |
| Mind control | Miseducation | Misfortunes |
| Mishaps | Mistreatment | Mistrust |
| Misunderstandings | Money laundering | Murder |
| Mutilation | National degradation | Obstinacy |
| Oppression | Pantheism | Perplexity |
| Persecution complex | Perversion | Perverted imaginations |
| Physical abuse | Pornography | Poverty |
| Prejudice | Premature death | Pride |
| Prohibitions | Prostitution | Provocation |

| | | |
|---|---|---|
| Psychic confusion | Psychological bondage | Psychological conditioning |
| Psychological games | Psychological rape | Racial cleansing |
| Racial profiling | Railing | Rape |
| Rationalization | Rebellion | Rejection |
| Religious spirit | Repressed Anger | Repression |
| Repudiation | Resentment | Resistance |
| Resolutions | Ridicule | Rulings |
| Sabotage | Sanctions | Satanic barriers |
| Scorn | Secularism | Sedition |
| Seduction | Segregation | Self-confidence |
| Self-hatred | Selfishness | Sexual abuse |
| Sexual dysfunction | Sexual harassment | Sexual slavery |
| Shame | Sickness | Sin |
| Single parenting | Slander | Slave trade |
| Slavery (all forms)** | Snares | Social conditioning |
| Social outcasts | Social rape | Soul ties |
| Spiritual abortions | Spiritual abuse | Spiritual adultery |
| Spiritual barrenness | Spiritual darkness | Spiritual erosion |
| Spiritual miscarriages | Spiritual bondage | Stigmas |
| Stigmatization | Strongholds | Stubbornness |
| Stumbling Blocks | Subliminal conditioning | Suicide |
| Suppression | Suppression of will | Surrogate parenting |
| Surveillance | Survival skills | Suspicion |
| Systemic lies | Threats | Torment |

| Traditional entrenchment | Traditions of man | Treachery |
|---|---|---|
| Under-employment | Undermining of rights | Unethical behavior |
| Unfair practices | Ungodly ambitions | Unholy desires |
| Vexation | Victimization | Violence |
| Vitiation of will | Wars | Weights |
| White-collar crime | Whoredom | Witchcraft |
| Willie lynchism | Worldliness | Wrath |
| Yoke | Unrighteous mammon | Longing for belonging |
| Poor self-perception | Poor nutritional habits | Repression of memories |
| Suppression of emotions | Suppression of expression | Perversions of thoughts |
| Calcification of the heart | Political disenfranchisement | Deviant patterns of behavior |
| Language disintegration | Inter-generational suspicions | Psychological conditioning |
| Male/female role reversal | Destabilization of the family | Invasions of personal privacy |
| Post-traumatic stress disorder | Catastrophication of situations | Suppression of genetic potential |
| Tyrannical governance/control | Inhuman conditions/treatment | Irrational thoughts and behaviors |
| Erosion of self-image and worth | Institutionalized homosexuality | Martyrdom of godly leadership |
| Diabolical proclivities and appetites | Independent female/dependent male | Artificial fabrication of consciousness |

| Bio-chemical altering techniques (fear, etc.) | Intergenerational proclivities and propensities | Eradication of personal/ethnical/national identity |
|---|---|---|
| Neurotic and psychotic behaviors and tendencies | Destruction of a sense of significance/identity/direction | Erosion and eradication of theocracy system and human rights |
| Social/emotional/psychological/temporal/spiritual/economical afflictions | Indifference of the oppressed to their circumstances and plight | |

**Release:** The hand of God, divine visitations, God's mercy, the arrows of God, righteousness to be exalted, national revival, soul-winning, the spirit of Elijah, the spirit of truth, the fear of Jehovah, salvation and deliverance, prophetic and apostolic anointing, the spirit of Jehu, the fear of the Lord, boldness, the rules of engagement, *Jehovah Gibbor*, legions of heavenly angels, kingdom of God and its principles and mandates, the anointing of evangelism and teaching.

# Spirit of Fear and Torment

THE SPIRIT OF fear is released to attack the peace, courage, vision and faith of individuals and creating a debilitating stronghold in their mind. It also has the power to abort purpose, derail divine destinies, and assassinate future hope and faith in the power of God. This is of extreme importance, to comprehend the insidious nature of this spirit relative to our future, because the way we perceive or think about the future actually sculpts and contours how we handle the present. Fear comes from the root word *phobos,* which connotes that which may cause flight. It is a psychological reaction to something or someone who poses a threat to our sense of security and safety. It also denotes emotional unrest and "dis-ease" caused by uncertainty of potency to overcome situations and life's challenges; financial, spiritual, physical, social, material, psychological, or emotional disability caused by demonic activities. Deuteronomy 2:25 indicates that fear is not only experienced on an individual basis, but also at a national level. God promises the Israelites that He will "begin to put the dread of thee and the fear of thee upon the nations that are under the whole heaven, who shall hear report of thee, and shall tremble, and be in anguish because of thee." Another word for fear is phobia, which is a persistent irrational fear of something that is so strong that it compels us to avoid the object of the fear.

There are different degrees of fear:

**Alarm:** Initial realization of danger

**Fright:** Sudden and momentary

**Dread:** Stronger in intensity, dread grips the heart as it anticipates impending events which are difficult or impossible to avoid, rendering the person helpless and powerless over it.

**Terror:** Overpowering, intense, and debilitating

**Horror:** A combination of fear and aversion

**Panic:** Sudden, frantic fear that robs a person of reason

**Dismay:** Apprehension that robs a person of courage and power to act efficiently and effectively

**Consternation:** A state of often paralyzing dismay characterized by confusion and helplessness

**Trepidation:** Dread characterized by trembling

For the thing which I greatly feared is come upon me, and that which I was afraid of is come unto me.
—JOB 3:25

Deliver me, I pray thee, from the hand of my brother, from the hand of Esau: for I fear him, lest he will come and smite me, and the mother with the children.
—GENESIS 32:11

For the LORD spake thus to me with a strong hand, and instructed me that I should not walk in the way of this people saying, Say ye not, A confederacy, to all them to whom this people shall say, A confederacy; neither fear ye their fear, nor be afraid. Sanctify the LORD of hosts himself; and let him be your fear, and let him be your dread. And he shall be for a sanctuary; but for a stone of stumbling and for a rock of offence to both the houses of Israel, for a gin and for a snare to the inhabitants of Jerusalem.

—ISAIAH 8:11–14

Then were the men exceedingly afraid, and said unto him, Why hast thou done this? For the men knew that he fled from the presence of the LORD, because he had told them.

—JONAH 1:10

Then let them which are in Judea flee to the mountains; and let them which are in the midst of it depart out; and let not them that are in the countries enter thereinto.

—LUKE 21:21

For ye have not received the spirit of bondage again to fear; but ye have received the Spirit of adoption, whereby we cry, Abba, Father.

—ROMANS 8:15

For God hath not given us the spirit of fear; but of power, and of love, and of a sound mind.

—2 TIMOTHY 1:7

There is no fear in love; but perfect love casteth out fear: because fear hath torment. He that feareth is not made perfect in love.

—1 JOHN 4:18

## Signs, Symptoms, and Manifestations of the Spirit of Fear and Torment

| | | |
|---|---|---|
| Nightmares | Inferiority | Fear of people |
| Insecurities | Oversensitivity | Insomnia |
| Fear of failure | Night-terrors | Phobias |
| Mistrust | Doubt | Anxiety |
| Nervousness | Depression | Extreme shyness |
| Pining | Loneliness | Fatalism |
| Crying | Shame | Condemnation |
| Terror | Heaviness | Fear of success |
| Alcoholism | Drug addiction | Criminal activities |
| Oppression | Deception | Witchcraft |
| Fear of people's opinions | Dread | Panic |
| Consternation | Horror | Tepidity |
| Alarm | Forgetfulness | Fear of change |
| Dismay | Discouragement | Disillusionment |
| Abuse | Control | Bondage |
| Agitation | Manipulation | Hostility |
| Treachery | Aversion | Victimization |
| Apprehension | Dismay | Acrophobia (fear of heights) |
| Aviaphobia (fear of flying) | Agoraphobia (fear of open spaces) | Apiphobia (fear of bees) |
| Amathophobia (fear of dust) | Astrophobia (fear of lightning) | Batrachophobia (fear of reptiles) |
| Blennophobia (fear of slime) | Claustrophobia (fear of enclosed spaces) | Cynophobia (fear of dogs) |

| | | |
|---|---|---|
| Decidophobia (fear of making decisions) | Electrophobia (fear of electricity) | Eremophobia (fear of being alone) |
| Gamophobia (fear of marriage) | Gatophobia (fear of cats) | Gephyrophobia (fear of crossing bridges) |
| Gynophobia (fear of women) | Hydrophobia (fear of water) | Kakorraphiaphobia (fear of failure) |
| Datagelophobia (fear of ridicule) | Deraunophobia (fear of thunder) | Musophobia (fear of mice) |
| Nyctophobia (fear of night) | Ochlophobia (fear of crowds) | Odynephobia (fear of pain) |
| Ophidiophobia (fear of snakes) | Pnigerophobia (fear of smothering) | Pyrophobia (fear of fire) |
| Scholionophobia (fear of school) | Sciophobia (fear of shadows) | Spermophobia (fear of germs) |
| Spheksophobia (fear of wasps) | Technophobia (fear of technology) | Thalassophobia (fear of the ocean) |
| Topophobia (fear of performing; stage fright) | Triskaidekaphobia (fear of the number thirteen) | Tropophobia (fear of moving or making changes) |
| Intimidation by adversary | | |

**Release:** Power, love, sound mind, boldness, peace, spiritual mindedness, liberty, and courage.

Thou shalt not be afraid for the terror by night; nor for the arrow that flieth by day.

—PSALM 91:5

### *Generational Curses*
See Spirits of Inheritance/Generational Curses (under Affinity)

### *Homosexuality*
See Perverse/Unclean

# Spirit of Idolatry

ONE OF THE works of the flesh, and a master spirit used by Satan to control corporal and corporate destinies, idolatry is the substitute for God/salvation. When you place anything or anyone ahead of God, and He is preempted as the zenith of pursuits and affection, this is idolatry. Idolatry has many modus operundi, such as social, natural, historical, spiritual, and cultural idolatry. The spirit of idolatry seduces people and nations to display extravagant emotional forms of the worship of things and/or people, while establishing strongholds of traditional, cultural practices and beliefs. Idolatry can manifest itself through philosophies, education and political activities and opens doors to demonic activities. According to Ezekiel, idolatry originates in the mind of Satan and projected into the minds of mankind:

> Then came certain of the elders of Israel unto me, and sat before me. And the word of the LORD came unto me, saying, Son of man, these men have set up their idols in their heart, and put the stumbling

block of their iniquity before their face: should I be inquired of at all by them? Therefore speak unto them, and say unto them, Thus saith the Lord GOD; Every man of the house of Israel that setteth up his idols in his heart, and putteth the stumblingblock of his iniquity before his face, and cometh to the prophet; I the LORD will answer him that cometh according to the multitude of his idols; That I may take the house of Israel in their own heart, because they are all estranged from me through their idols. Therefore say unto the house of Israel, Thus saith the Lord GOD; Repent, and turn yourselves from your idols; and turn away your faces from all your abominations. For every one of the house of Israel, or of the stranger that sojourneth in Israel, which separateth himself from me, and setteth up his idols in his heart, and putteth the stumblingblock of his iniquity before his face, and cometh to a prophet to inquire of him concerning me; I the LORD will answer him by myself: And I will set my face against that man, and will make him a sign and a proverb, and I will cut him off from the midst of my people; and ye shall know that I am the LORD.

—EZEKIEL 14:1–8

For rebellion is as the sin of witchcraft, and stubbornness is as iniquity and idolatry. Because thou hast rejected the word of the LORD, he hath also rejected thee from being king.

—1 SAMUEL 15:23

What profiteth the graven image that the maker thereof hath graven it; the molten image, and a teacher of lies, that the maker of his work trusteth therein, to make dumb idols?

—HABAKKUK 2:18

Ye know that ye were Gentiles, carried away unto these dumb idols, even as ye were led.

—1 CORINTHIANS 12:2

Idolatry, witchcraft, hatred, variance, emulations, wrath, strife, seditions, [and] heresies.

—GALATIANS 5:20

Mortify therefore your members which are upon the earth; fornication, uncleanness, inordinate affection, evil concupiscence, and covetousness, which is idolatry.

—COLOSSIANS 3:5

| Signs, Symptoms, and Manifestations of the Spirit of Idolatry | | |
|---|---|---|
| Religiosity | Covetousness | Greed |
| Control | Inordinate affection | Fornication |
| Impurities | Doctrines of devils | Humanism |
| False worship | Witchcraft | Uncleanness |
| Immoralities | Perversion | Self-centeredness |
| Astrology | Cultic practices | False prophecies |
| Pride | Narcissism | Carnality |
| Murder | Heresies | Fear |
| Oppression | Possession | Confusion |
| Unbelief | Knowledge block | Evil desires |
| Evil thoughts | Lust | Enticement |

| Entanglement | Degradation | Error |
|---|---|---|
| Enslavement of emotion | National/ ethnical traits, tendencies, and oddities | |

**Release:** True/pure worship (in spirit and truth), righteousness, holiness, repentance, and prophetic anointing.

# Spirits of Jealousy and Envy

IN THIS SECTION, we will explore two spirits that the average people view as being one and the same. Normally, we tend to use the words *jealousy* and *envy* interchangeably, when in fact, although they exist on the same continuum, they are on opposite ends. Let us first examine the spirit of jealousy.

The Bible states that jealousy is as cruel as the grave. What a way to describe the resentful desire for a person's drive to gain an advantage in life at the expense of another. Jealous is a spirit that will cause a person who possesses something he perceives as valuable to not want anyone else to have it or enjoy it; for example: if a person has a relationship with someone powerful and influential, or he possesses information, a car, or a home in an exclusive area, and he wants to enjoy this ownership exclusively, that person is considered a jealous person. That is to say, he does not want anyone else to enjoy a relationship with him or access the same information, own a similar car or home, or enjoy other pleasures and amenities similar to his. The person who enjoys that relationship or other possessions will do all he can to ensure no one else gets that same opportunity, even to the point of withholding information and will plot, plan, sabotage (see the section *Sabotage* for further explanation), and undermine to ensure that the other person does not have similar privileges. You may ask the question, "Doesn't Scripture view God as a jealous God?" Exodus 34:14 states: "For thou shalt worship no other god: for the LORD, whose name is Jealous, is a jealous God," and Deuteronomy 4:24 declares: "For the LORD thy God is a consuming fire, even a jealous God." Using this scripture to define jealousy makes our task even simpler. Since God possesses everything, His jealousy simply stated means that He does not want anyone to have what belongs to Him, and that He is not willing to share it with anyone else. On the other hand, we are mere stewards of what really belongs to God. Therefore, we do not have the right to say what another person can or cannot enjoy. Do you see how jealousy operates? God has a right to do whatever He wants with what He owns. But we cannot dictate to God who should or should not have the right or privilege to enjoy what He allows people to enjoy. Nabal is a biblical character that comes to mind of how a jealous person operates.

> And Samuel died; and all the Israelites were gathered together, and lamented him, and buried him in his house at Ramah. And David arose, and went down to the wilderness of Paran. And there was a man in Maon, whose possessions were in Carmel; and the man was very great, and he had three thousand sheep, and a thousand goats: and he was shearing his sheep in Carmel. Now the name of the man was Nabal; and

the name of his wife Abigail: and she was a woman of good understanding, and of a beautiful countenance: but the man was churlish and evil in his doings; and he was of the house of Caleb. And David heard in the wilderness that Nabal did shear his sheep. And David sent out ten young men, and David said unto the young men, Get you up to Carmel, and go to Nabal, and greet him in my name: And thus shall ye say to him that liveth in prosperity, Peace be both to thee, and peace be to thine house, and peace be unto all that thou hast. And now I have heard that thou hast shearers: now thy shepherds which were with us, we hurt them not, neither was there ought missing unto them, all the while they were in Carmel. Ask thy young men, and they will shew thee. Wherefore let the young men find favour in thine eyes: for we come in a good day: give, I pray thee, whatsoever cometh to thine hand unto thy servants, and to thy son David. And when David's young men came, they spake to Nabal according to all those words in the name of David, and ceased. And Nabal answered David's servants, and said, Who is David? and who is the son of Jesse? there be many servants now a days that break away every man from his master. Shall I then take my bread, and my water, and my flesh that I have killed for my shearers, and give it unto men, whom I know not whence they be? So David's young men turned their way, and went again, and came and told him all those sayings. And David said unto his men, Gird ye on every man his sword. And they girded on every man his sword; and David also girded on his sword: and there went up after David about four hundred men; and two hundred abode by the stuff. But one of the young men told Abigail, Nabal's wife, saying, Behold, David sent messengers out of the wilderness to salute our master; and he railed on them. But the men were very good unto us, and we were not hurt, neither missed we any thing, as long as we were conversant with them, when we were in the fields: They were a wall unto us both by night and day, all the while we were with them keeping the sheep. Now therefore know and consider what thou wilt do; for evil is determined against our master, and against all his household: for he is such a son of Belial, that a man cannot speak to him.

—1 SAMUEL 25:1–17

Jealousy is likened unto a raging fire, which is out of control and destroys everything it touches. Jealous people are destructive people. They are also possessive people. They smother and are overly possessive of everything and everyone. Jealousy is the opposite of zeal. The Bible talks of zeal as a passion that drives man to accomplish great things for Him. Jealousy on the other hand will drive man to accomplish things that are contrary to the will of God.

Let's look at a familiar scenario that occurred in Scripture. Saul was seated in an influential position in Israel as king. However, God anointed David to replace him. This move of God caused him to become jealous, and he did everything to keep David out of his position and seat of authority. His jealousy led him to conspire against David.

Envy, on the other hand, is slightly different from jealousy. According to *American Heritage Dictionary*, envy is defined as a feeling of discontent and resentment aroused by and in conjunction with desire for the possessions or qualities of another. Envy will have you thinking that the grass is greener on the other side. For instance, it will convince you that other people are so much more luckier, smarter, more attractive, better off than you, more educated, or enjoy better relationships. Envy, therefore, is the desire for others' traits, status, abilities, or situations. Most people tend to use the word envy and jealousy interchangeably, but there is a difference. Envy is wanting what someone else has while jealousy is not wanting someone to have or enjoy what you have. Jealous and envious people are insecure people.

# Jealousy

For jealousy is the rage of a man: therefore he will not spare in the day of vengeance.

—PROVERBS 6:34

Set me as a seal upon thine heart, as a seal upon thine arm: for love is strong as death; jealousy is cruel as the grave: the coals thereof are coals of fire, which hath a most vehement flame.

—SONG OF SOLOMON 8:6

And it came to pass in the sixth year, in the sixth month, in the fifth day of the month, as I sat in mine house, and the elders of Judah sat before me, that the hand of the Lord GOD fell there upon me. Then I beheld, and lo a likeness as the appearance of fire: from the appearance of his loins even downward, fire; and from his loins even upward, as the appearance of brightness, as the colour of amber. And he put forth the form of an hand, and took me by a lock of mine head; and the spirit lifted me up between the earth and the heaven, and brought me in the visions of God to Jerusalem, to the door of the inner gate that looketh toward the north; where was the seat of the image of jealousy, which provoketh to jealousy. And, behold, the glory of the God of Israel was there, according to the vision that I saw in the plain. Then said he unto me, Son of man, lift up thine eyes now the way toward the north. So I lifted up mine eyes the way toward the north, and behold northward at the gate of the altar this image of jealousy in the entry. He said furthermore unto me, Son of man, seest thou what they do? even the great abominations that the house of Israel committeth here, that I should go far off from my sanctuary? but turn thee yet again, and thou shalt see greater abominations. And he brought me to the door of the court; and when I looked, behold a hole in the wall. Then said he unto me, Son of man, dig now in the wall: and when I had digged in the wall, behold a door. And he said unto me, Go in, and behold the wicked abominations that they do here. So I went in and saw; and behold every form of creeping things, and abominable beasts, and all the idols of the house of Israel, pourtrayed upon the wall round about. And there stood before them seventy men of the ancients of the house of Israel, and in the midst of them stood Jaazaniah the son of Shaphan, with every man his censer in his hand; and a thick cloud of incense went up. Then said he unto me, Son of man, hast thou seen what the ancients of the house of Israel do in the dark, every man in the chambers of his imagery? for they say, The LORD seeth us not; the LORD hath forsaken the earth.

—EZEKIEL 8:1–12

## Envy

For wrath killeth the foolish man, and envy slayeth the silly one.

—JOB 5:2

Envy thou not the oppressor, and choose none of his ways.

—PROVERBS 3:31

A sound heart is the life of the flesh: but envy the rottenness of the bones.

—PROVERBS 14:30

Let not thine heart envy sinners: but be thou in the fear of the LORD all the day long.

—PROVERBS 23:17

Wrath is cruel, and anger is outrageous; but who is able to stand before envy?

—PROVERBS 27:4

In the following text, you will observe the spirit of envy and jealous at work in King Saul. Even though Saul was given great citations and accolades for his feats, he wanted all the attention to be placed upon him. As soon as a bit of attention was given to David, both spirits seized his heart.

And David went out whithersoever Saul sent him, and behaved himself wisely: and Saul set him over the men of war, and he was accepted in the sight of all the people, and also in the sight of Saul's servants. And it came to pass as they came, when David was returned from the slaughter of the Philistine, that the women came out of all cities of Israel, singing and dancing, to meet king Saul, with tabrets, with joy, and with instruments of musick. And the women answered one another as they played, and said, Saul hath slain his thousands, and David his ten thousands. And Saul was very wroth, and the saying displeased him; and he said, they have ascribed unto David ten thousands, and to me they have ascribed but thousands: and what can he have more but the kingdom? And Saul eyed David from that day and forward. And it came to pass on the morrow, that the evil spirit from God came upon Saul, and he prophesied in the midst of the house: and David played with his hand, as at other times: and there was a javelin in Saul's hand. And Saul cast the javelin; for he said, I will smite David even to the wall with it. And David avoided out of his presence twice.

—1 SAMUEL 18:5–11

| Signs, Symptoms, and Manifestations of the Spirits of Jealousy and Envy | | |
| --- | --- | --- |
| Seditions | Cursing | Railing |
| Gossip | Contention | Lying |
| Belittlement | Maligning ways | Violence |
| Derision | Criticism | Mocking |
| "Keeping up with the Joneses" | Sabotage | Babylon |

| | | |
|---|---|---|
| Rejection | Begrudging attitude | Murder |
| Character assassination | Ill wishes | Ill-spoken words |
| Strife | Taunt | Threats |
| Resentment | Slander | Discord |
| Spite | Malice | Ill will |
| Extreme competition | Covetousness | Undermining (purpose) |
| Rage | Deception | Withholding information |
| Nonsupportiveness | Idolatry | Arrogance |
| Pride | Insecurity | Lust |
| Self-centeredness | Greed | Theft |
| Embezzlement | Identity theft | Fear |
| Projection | Frustration | Confusion |
| Pain | Torment | Obsession |
| Agony | Surveillance | Entitlement |
| Possessiveness | Manipulation | Assumptions |
| Idolatry | Justification | Abuse |
| Bullying | Misrepresentation of truth | Lying |
| Witchcraft | Oppression | Jezebel |
| Beliel | | |

**Release:** Brotherly love, kindness, meekness, respect, celebration, and satisfaction.

# Spirit of Jezebel (Anarchy, Control, and Witchcraft)

MANY PEOPLE BELIEVE the Jezebel spirit is a matriarchal leadership. For instance, when a man dies and leaves his wife behind with children, the woman will assume the role of the head of the house. This does not mean she is usurping authority. Instead, she assumes the role of authority head. During the judgeship of Deborah the nation of Israel existed under a matriarchal spirit.

What God does despise is anarchy; this is the spirit of Jezebel. This spirit is pious, puffed up with pride, and blatantly disregards delegated authority. It works contrary to the laws of spiritual protocol. This spirit, puffed up with pride, refuses to submit. Instead, it rallies for the authority and influence that rightfully belongs to God's appointed leadership. A Jezebel spirit operates both through males and females, and appeals to the iniquity of the heart often utilizing "Ahab" to fulfill her wishes and desires. Failure to oblige or obey her will cause this spirit to retaliate violently. A Jezebel spirit hates the prophetic, holiness, righteousness; and it plots and plans the demise of delegated authority.

There are two distinct manifestations of the spirit of Jezebel spoken of in Scripture. The first found in 1 Kings is assigned to prophets, and the other reference is found in the Book of Revelation and is assigned to masquerade as a prophet. The name Jezebel means unmarried. Every child of God is "married" to Jehovah. We are his *brides*. Jezebel operates in the flesh and is guilty of fornication and harlotry. This spirit drives its host to commit spiritual fornication, consistently conceiving "bastard" children for Satan: her lover. This spirit is powerful because it can marshal satanic cohorts at a single command. (See also The Spirit of Divination)

| Signs, Symptoms, and Manifestations of the Spirit of Jezebel | | |
|---|---|---|
| 1 Kings 18:21–25 | | |
| 2 Kings 9 (works against the prophetic) | | |
| Lust for power | Spirit of control | Idolatry |
| Hatred of authority | Witchcraft | Manipulation |
| Abominations | Sexual sins | Deception |
| Hidden agenda | Blasphemy | Factions |
| Maligning of character | Sedition | Rebellion |
| Contention | Paranoia | Vanity |
| Overconfidence | Opinionated | Suspicion |
| Adultery (sexual/spiritual) | Persecution | Irreverence |
| Lustful affections | Jealousy | Anarchy |

| | | |
|---|---|---|
| Usurping authority | Insubordination | Insecurity |
| Mind control | Violence | Retaliation |
| Harassment | Hatred | Envy |
| Railing (verbal abuse) | Bitterness | Anger |
| Competition | Spirit of fear | Spirit of rejection |
| Slander | Surveillance | Prohibition of potential |
| Spiritual whoredom | Beliel | Insecurity protected by pride |
| Ahab | Frustrating growth and maturation process | Physical restraints/ constraints |
| Showing displeasure (facially, emotionally, verbally) | Revelation 2:18–29 (prophetic counterfeit) | False deceptive anointing |
| Heresy | Self-appointment | Apathy |
| Usurping authority | Control | Compromise |
| Seduction | Carnality | Fornication |
| Arrogance | Self-sufficiency | Lack of faith in God |
| Spiritual fornication | Works of the flesh | False teaching |
| False doctrine (of men) | Witchcraft | Satanic and demonic activities |
| "Religious Holiness" | | |

**Confess:** Sins of father, command curses to be lifted from person and descendants.

**Release:** Repentance, holiness, godliness, the anointing, prophetic anointing, humility, spirit of Elijah and Jehu, gift of discerning of spirits, righteousness, fire of the Lord, terror of the Lord, breaking the curse of whoredom, order the veils of curses, deception, and control to be torn down and ripped to shreds; break chains and soulish ties.

# Spirit of Judas

THIS SPIRIT IS assigned to "movers and shakers" in the kingdom (those who are like Jesus) to violate allegiance to them. They give aid and information to the enemies of the one to whom they are assigned. In the military, a *sleeper* is one who has undercover, surreptitious assignments. He looks, acts, talks, and walks like "one of us," but has an assignment from another camp. This spirit can remain undercover and undetected for years before they strike.

> Then Judas, which betrayed him, answered and said, Master, is it I? He said unto him, Thou hast said.
> —MATTHEW 26:25

| Signs, Symptoms, and Manifestations of the Spirit of Judas | | |
| --- | --- | --- |
| Filthy lucre (love of money) | Sabotage | Deception |
| Lust | Worldliness | Noncommittal |

| Double-mindedness | Betrayal | Treason |
|---|---|---|
| Treachery | Sedition | Disloyalty |
| Double-crossing | Duplicity | Unfaithfulness |
| Foul play | Faithlessness | Falseness |
| Traitorship | Infidelity | Fraud |

**Release:** Order, protocol, humility, unity, the mind of Christ, submission, hope, faith, fidelity, trustworthiness, and faithfulness.

# Spirit of Korah (Rebellion)

THIS SPIRIT CAUSES insurrection to arise within the ranks of leadership. It is a spirit that forms unholy alliances and convinces leadership to rebel against divine and delegated authority (i.e. pastors, eldership). It refuses to give honor and respect to whom it is due because it causes its hosts to feel that they are equal in status, station, and call. This spirit is like a cancer that quickly spreads within a local church. In order to eliminate the contamination within the ranks of leadership, this spirit must be openly challenged, judged, and forcefully expelled.

Now Korah, the son of Izhar, the son of Kohath, the son of Levi, and Dathan and Abiram, the sons of Eliab, and On, the son of Peleth, sons of Reuben, took men: And they rose up before Moses, with certain of the children of Israel, two hundred and fifty princes of the assembly, famous in the congregation, men of renown: And they gathered themselves together against Moses and against Aaron, and said unto them, Ye take too much upon you, seeing all the congregation are holy, every one of them, and the LORD is among them: wherefore then lift ye up yourselves above the congregation of the LORD? And when Moses heard it, he fell upon his face: And he spake unto Korah and unto all his company, saying, Even to morrow the LORD will shew who are his, and who is holy; and will cause him to come near unto him: even him whom he hath chosen will he cause to come near unto him. This do; Take you censers, Korah, and all his company; And put fire therein, and put incense in them before the LORD to morrow: and it shall be that the man whom the Lord doth choose, he shall be holy: ye take too much upon you, ye sons of Levi. And Moses said unto Korah, Hear, I pray you, ye sons of Levi: Seemeth it but a small thing unto you, that the God of Israel hath separated you from the congregation of Israel, to bring you near to himself to do the service of the tabernacle of the LORD, and to stand before the congregation to minister unto them? And he hath brought thee near to him, and all thy brethren the sons of Levi with thee: and seek ye the priesthood also? For which cause both thou and all thy company are gathered together against the LORD: and what is Aaron, that ye murmur against him? And Moses sent to call Dathan and Abiram, the sons of Eliab: which said, We will not come up: Is it a small thing that thou hast brought us up out of a land that floweth with milk and honey, to kill us in the wilderness, except thou make thyself altogether a prince over us? Moreover thou hast not brought us into a land that floweth with milk and honey, or given us inheritance of fields and vineyards: wilt thou put out the eyes of these men? we will not come up. And Moses was very wroth, and said unto the LORD, Respect not thou their offering: I have not taken one ass from them, neither have I hurt one of them. And Moses said unto Korah, Be thou and all thy company before the LORD, thou, and they, and Aaron, to morrow: And take every man his censer, and put incense in them, and bring ye before the LORD every man his censer, two hundred and fifty censers; thou also, and Aaron, each of you his censer. And they took every man his censer, and put fire in them, and laid incense thereon, and stood in the door of the tabernacle of the congregation with Moses and Aaron. And Korah gathered all the congregation against them unto the door of the tabernacle of the congregation: and the glory of the LORD appeared unto all the congregation.

—NUMBERS 16:1–19

| Signs, Symptoms, and Manifestations of the Spirit of Korah | | |
|---|---|---|
| Presumption | Rivalry | Disrespect |
| Judgmental attitude | Disrespect for protocol | Arrogance |
| Hostility | Fault-finding | Railing |
| Accusation | Corruption | Iniquitous hearts |
| Confrontation | Power struggle | Divide and conquer |
| Power hunger | Disillusionment | Rebellion |

| Revolt against leadership | Sabotage | Undermining authority |
|---|---|---|
| Deceit | Ministerial curse | Backsliding of parishioners |
| Cultural curse | Loss of confidence in spiritual leadership | |

**Release:** Order, protocol, humility, unity, and the mind of Christ, submission, hope, faith, and longsuffering.

# Spirit of Madness or
# Mental Illness

I WANT TO HANDLE this category as sensitively as possible because of other medical and contributing factors. However, in as much as I am aware that there are certain conditions that can be caused by spirits of oppression, I am equally aware that God does not place any form of illness upon us. This is not to imply that the enemy has possessed everyone who displays characteristics of mental illness. I am saying that we need to place the blame on the character from which these unfortunate conditions emanates: Satan himself.

The Book of Revelation 18:11–13 states, "And the merchants of the earth shall weep and mourn over her [Babylon]; for no man buyeth their merchandise any more: The merchandise of gold, and silver, and precious stones, and of pearls, and fine linen, and purple, and silk, and scarlet, and all thyine wood, and all manner vessels of ivory, and all manner vessels of most precious wood, and of brass, and iron, and marble, And

209

cinnamon, and odours, and ointments, and frankincense, and wine, and oil, and fine flour, and wheat, and beasts, and sheep, and horses, and chariots, and slaves, and souls of men."

This text speaks of Satan utilizing the mental capacity of man to fulfill his plans and purposes in the earth realm. One of the ways he utilizes the minds of men is to create mental disorders, irrational, obsessive behaviors, impairing the capacity to function adequately and appropriately. The National Alliance for the Mentally Ill defines mental illness as "a group of disorders causing severe disturbances in thinking, feeling, and relating" which diminishes one's ability to cope with normal demands. Common mental and emotional difficulties include anxiety disorders, substance abuse, Alzheimer's disease, and phobias. Brief descriptions of some of the most common illnesses is as follows:

**Alzheimer's Disease:** A degenerative disorder; one of the most prominent types of dementia.

**Anxiety:** An emotional state having no recognizable source marked by fear and apprehension.

**Autism:** Severe developmental disorder marked by difficulties in communications and relationships.

**Bipolar Disorder:** A "disease that pitches patients from depressed to hyperactive and euphoric, or intensely irritable," says Kay Redfield Jamison, psychiatry professor at Johns Hopkins University School of Medicine.

**Delusions:** Fixed false beliefs that can't be changed by rational arguments.

**Dementia:** Disorder with memory loss, deterioration in personal care, and impaired reasoning.

**Depression:** Emotional disturbance varying from "the blues" to paralyzing hopelessness.

**Hallucinations:** Seeing, hearing, tasting, touching, or smelling something not real.

**Obsessive Compulsive Disorder (OCD):** Persistent unwanted thoughts and repetitive behaviors.

**Panic Disorder:** Attacks with symptoms such as shortness of breath, trembling, and terror.

**Phobia:** Pathologically strong, inappropriate fear of an ordinary event or thing. See *Fear* for more details.

**Post-Traumatic Stress Disorder (PTSD):** After effects, i.e., flashbacks and nightmares, sometimes long after someone has had a severe shock.

**Psychosis:** Severe mental disorder with loss of contact with reality, hallucinations, and delusions.

**Seasonal Affective Disorder (SAD):** "Winter depression" linked to seasonal decrease in daylight.

**Schizophrenia:** A group of disorders marked by delusions, hallucinations, and disorganized thinking. Taken from the Greek meaning "splitting of the mind," connections between what is going on within the person and what is happening in the outside world seem to split apart. Schizophrenia usually shows up in one's teen years, twenties, or early thirties.

And they came over unto the other side of the sea, into the country of the Gadarenes. And when he was come out of the ship, immediately there met him out of the tombs a man with an unclean spirit, Who had his dwelling among the tombs; and no man could bind him, no, not with chains: Because that he had been often bound with fetters and chains, and the chains had been plucked asunder by him, and the fetters broken in pieces: neither could any man tame him. And always, night and day, he was in the mountains, and in the tombs, crying, and cutting himself with stones. But when he saw Jesus afar off, he ran and worshipped him, And cried with a loud voice, and said, What have I to do with thee, Jesus, thou Son of the most high God? I adjure thee by God, that thou torment me not. For he said unto him, Come out of the man, thou unclean spirit. And he asked him, What is thy name? And he answered, saying, My name is Legion: for we are many. And he besought him much that he would not send them away out of the country. Now there was there nigh unto the mountains a great herd of swine feeding. And all the devils besought him, saying, Send us into the swine, that we may enter into them. And forthwith Jesus gave them leave. And the unclean spirits went out, and entered into the swine; and the herd ran violently down a steep place into the sea, (they were about two thousand;) and were choked in the sea. And they that fed the swine fled, and told it in the city, and in the country. And they went out to see what it was that was done. And they come to Jesus, and see him that was possessed with the devil, and had the legion, sitting, and clothed, and in his right mind: and they were afraid. And they that saw it told them how it befell to him that was possessed with the devil, and also concerning the swine. And they began to pray him to depart out of their coasts. And when he was come into the ship, he that had been possessed with the devil prayed him that he might be with him. Howbeit Jesus suffered him not, but saith unto him, Go home to thy friends, and tell them how great things the Lord hath done for thee, and hath had compassion on thee. And he departed, and began to publish in Decapolis how great things Jesus had done for him: and all men did marvel.

—MARK 5:1–20

## Signs, Symptoms, and Manifestations of the Spirit of Madness, or Mental Illness

| | | |
|---|---|---|
| Schizophrenia | Memory loss/recall | Confusion |
| Irrational thoughts | Dementia | Poor recall |
| Oppression | Nervousness | Inferiority complex |
| Hysteria | Compulsive behavior | Melancholy |
| Dread | Paranoia | Addictions |
| Mistrust | Unworthiness | Senility |
| Mutilation | Neurosis | Sociopath conditions |
| Murder | Worry | Phobias |
| Magical thinking | Fear | Inordinate withdrawal |
| Personality disorders | Uncontrolled crying | Delusional projections |
| Depression | Death | Persecutory paranoid state |
| Bi-polar | Dependent disorder | Mental illness |
| Craziness | Derangement | Alienation |
| Lunacy | Insanity | Mania |
| Obsessiveness | Violence | Shame |
| Terror | Possessiveness | Lack of motivation |

| Hypersensitivity | Perfectionism | Grandiosity |
|---|---|---|
| Psychosis | Embarrassment | Suppression |
| Phobia | Panic disorder | |
| "Blues" | Feeling down | Alzheimer |
| Psychosomatic illness | Overcompensation disorder | Mental/ psychological oppression |

**Release:** Love, the mind of Christ, restoration, healing, deliverance, and peace.

# Spirit of Murder

THIS SPIRIT WORKS with the six spirits of the underworld. It seeks to cause premature death as it unlawfully takes a person's right to live.

> He sitteth in the lurking places of the villages: in the secret places doth he murder the innocent: his eyes are privily set against the poor.
>
> —PSALM 10:8

> For out of the heart proceed evil thoughts, murders, adulteries, fornications, thefts, false witness, blasphemies.
>
> —MATTHEW 15:19

| Signs, Symptoms, and Manifestations of the Spirit of Murder | | |
|---|---|---|
| Suicide | Infanticide | Fratricide |
| Homicide | Slander | Abortion |
| Gossip | Violence | Victimization |

| Spirit of Herod | Spirit of Pharaoh | Mutilation |
|---|---|---|
| Intimidation | Fear | Terror |
| Emotional/psychological rape | Assassination | Execution |
| Manslaughter | Persecution | Scandal |
| Stigmatization | Character assassination | Sabotage |

**Release:** The mind of Christ, faith, hope, love, life in Christ Jesus, the anointing, the spirit of resurrection, and the spirit of Elijah.

# Spirit of Nabal

THE NAME NABAL is literally translated vile, stupid, or foolish. Scripture states that he was churlish. Nabal's name in Hebrew is *qaheh*. It literally means cruel, impudent, and rough. You may know people who, no matter how kindly they are treated, never reciprocate with kindness. They walk around as if they have a chip on their shoulders and are mad at the whole world.

And there was a man in Maon, whose possessions were in Carmel; and the man was very great, and he had three thousand sheep, and a thousand goats: and he was shearing his sheep in Carmel. Now the name of the man was Nabal; and the name of his wife Abigail: and she was a woman of good understanding, and of a beautiful countenance: but the man was churlish and evil in his doings; and he was of the house of Caleb. And David heard in the wilderness that Nabal did shear his sheep. And David sent out ten young men, and David said unto the young men, Get you up to Carmel, and go to Nabal, and greet him in my name: And thus shall ye say to him that liveth in prosperity, Peace be both to thee, and peace be to thine house, and peace be unto all that thou hast. And now I have heard that thou hast shearers: now thy shepherds which were with us, we hurt them not, neither was there ought missing unto them, all the while they were in Carmel. Ask thy young men, and they will shew thee. Wherefore let the young men find favour in thine eyes: for we come in a good day: give, I pray thee, whatsoever cometh to thine hand unto thy servants, and to thy son David. And when David's young men came, they spake to Nabal according to all those words in the name of David, and ceased. And Nabal answered David's servants, and said, Who is David? and who is the son of Jesse? there be many servants now a days that break away every man from his master. Shall I then take my bread, and my water, and my flesh that I have killed for my shearers, and give it unto men, whom I know not whence they be?

—1 SAMUEL 25:2–11

| Signs, Symptoms, and Manifestations of the Spirit of Nabal | | |
|---|---|---|
| Disrespect for authority | Dishonor | Irreverence |
| Churlishness | Difficult personality | Impudence |
| Vulgarity | Disrespect | Harassment |
| Stinginess | Noncompliance | Obstinacy |
| Insensibility | Cruelty | Hardness |

| Stiff-neck | Hard-heartedness | Selfishness |
|---|---|---|
| Stubbornness | Sorrowful | Abuse |
| Severity | Indifference | Grief |
| Insubordination | Disinterest | Lethargy |
| Disregard | Apathy | |

**Release:** Humility, cooperation, peace, mercy, and patience.

# Spirit of Oppression

WORKING IN CONJUNCTION with the spirit of Pharaoh, the spirit of Oppression arbitrarily exercises satanic powers to oppress and cause mental and emotional stress. It victimizes its host of his rights and dignity. This spirit also creates a "slave" mentality, that even after a person is delivered from the clutches of its relentless hands, the individual must be exposed to empowering teachings so as to cause a paradigm shift.

> Thou shalt not oppress an hired servant that is poor and needy, whether he be of thy brethren, or of thy strangers that are in thy land within thy gates: At his day thou shalt give him his hire, neither shall the sun go down upon it; for he is poor, and setteth his heart upon it: lest he cry against thee unto the LORD, and it be sin unto thee.
>
> —DEUTERONOMY 24:14–15

For he hath not despised nor abhorred the affliction of the afflicted; neither hath he hid his face from him; when he cried unto him, he heard.... Turn thee unto me, and have mercy upon me; for I am desolate and afflicted.

—Psalm 22:24; 25:16

Give ear to my prayer, O God, and hide not thyself from my supplication. Attend unto me, and hear me: I mourn in my complaint, and make a noise; Because of the voice of the enemy, because of the oppression of the wicked: for they cast iniquity upon me, and in wrath they hate me. My heart is sore pained within me: and the terrors of death are fallen upon me. Fearfulness and trembling are come upon me, and horror hath overwhelmed me. And I said, Oh that I had wings like a dove! For then would I fly away, and be at rest. Lo, then would I wander far off, and remain in the wilderness. Selah. I would hasten my escape from the windy storm and tempest. Destroy, O Lord, and divide their tongues: for I have seen violence and strife in the city. Day and night they go about it upon the walls thereof: mischief also and sorrow are in the midst of it. Wickedness is in the midst thereof: deceit and guile depart not from her streets. For it was not an enemy that reproached me; then I could have borne it: neither was it he that hated me that did magnify himself against me; then I would have hid myself from him: But it was thou, a man mine equal, my guide, and mine acquaintance. We took sweet counsel together, and walked unto the house of God in company. Let death seize upon them, and let them go down quick into hell: for wickedness is in their dwellings, and among them.

—PSALM 55:1–15

The spirit of a man will sustain his infirmity; but a wounded spirit who can bear?

—PROVERBS 18:14

How God anointed Jesus of Nazareth with the Holy Ghost and with power: who went about doing good, and healing all that were oppressed of the devil; for God was with him.

—ACTS 10:38

## Signs, Symptoms, and Manifestations of the Spirit of Oppresssion

| | | |
|---|---|---|
| Discouragement | Despondency | Despair |
| Hopelessness | Heaviness | Defeatism |
| Depression | Chronic weariness | Poverty |
| Confusion | Insomnia | Lack of motivation |
| Lack of direction | Emotional pain | Nervousness |
| Breakdowns | Lack/loss of appetite | Night fears/terrors |
| Fatalism | Condemnation | Inferiority complex |
| Harassment | Apathy | Stress |
| Subjugation of hope | Knowledge block | Slavery |
| Repression | Communism | Eating disorders |
| Helplessness | Disunity | Domination of will |
| Psychological enslavement | Spirit of Herod | Loneliness |

| Beliel | Jezebel | Behemoth |
| --- | --- | --- |
| Leviathan | Herod | Pharaoh |
| Lack of connectedness | False/nonexpectations | Sabotage of potential |
| Undermining of purpose | Longing for belonging | Incarceration of motivation |
| Enslavement of emotions | Language deterioration/disintegration | Social/political disenfranchisement |
| Entrapment of perception | Erosion of self-esteem/image | Suppression of expression |
| Post-traumatic stress disorder | Invasion of personal privacy | Self-fulfilling prophecies |
| Catastrophication of situations | Creation of subcultures (social outcasts) | Prohibition of fulfillment of personal purpose |
| Eradication of personal/ethical/national identity | Destruction of a sense of significance/identity and direction | Social, emotional, psychological, temporal, spiritual afflictions |
| Inability to respond appropriately to challenges, conflict, or crises | | |

**Release:** Deliverance, apostolic anointing, prophetic anointing, peace, healing, mercy, and liberty.

See the Spirit of Egypt/Pharaoh/Herod.

# Spirit of Perversion

THIS SPIRIT THAT causes an individual or groups of people to deviate from what is moral, ethical, right, and good. Working with an unclean spirit, it causes its host to obstinately persist in an error or a fault. Many individuals plagued, tormented, oppressed, or possessed with this spirit will be wrongly and strongly self-willed or stubborn, and marked by a disposition that opposes and contradicts. This English word comes from the Hebrew root word *aqash,* which has the connotation of being twisted and distorted; thus the English words *false, crooked, froward,* and *perverse.*

> They have corrupted themselves, their spot is not the spot of his children: they are a perverse and crooked generation.
>
> —DEUTERONOMY 32:5

> Whoso walketh uprightly shall be saved: but he that is perverse in his ways shall fall at once.
>
> —PROVERBS 28:18

## Signs, Symptoms, and Manifestations of the Spirit of Perversion

| | | |
|---|---|---|
| Adultery | Nymphomania | Treachery |
| Bestiality | Seduction | Falsehood |
| Bitterness | Corruption | Lying |
| Unnatural affections | Sodomy | Exhibitionism |
| Child abuse | Rape | Exaggeration |
| Chronic promiscuity | Fetishism | Religious |
| Debauchery | Lesbianism | Cursing |
| Dishonesty | Inordinate affections | Uncleanness |
| Divination | Rebellion | Witchcraft |
| Effeminacy | Deceit | Gossip |
| Fornication | Prostitution | Zoophilia |
| Lusts of every kind | Deception | Imagination |
| Homosexuality | Guile | Immorality |
| Indecency | Masochism | Impure motives |
| Immoralities | Unethical dealings | Incest |
| Flirtation | Condemnation | Instability |
| Victimization | Manipulations | Paraphilia |
| Transvestitism | Profanity | Perversions |
| Vileness | Control | Pornography |
| Cannibalism | Vanity | Religiosity |
| Flattery | Voyeurism | Sadism |
| Filthy language | Filthy thoughts | Sexual perversions |
| Pedophilia | Sexual violence/ torture | Sexually explicit dreams |

| Railing | Slander | Accusation |
|---|---|---|
| Wrath | Stubbornness | Dogmatisms |
| Inflexibility | Cross-dressing | Provocative dressing |
| Drag-queen | Butchmism | Effeminism |
| Prostitution | | |

**Release:** Righteousness, holiness, self-control, deliverance, healing, the breaking of soul ties, and fruit of the Spirit, and discipline.

# Spirit of Poverty
## and Financial Curses

THIS SPIRIT CREATES an atmosphere of financial infertility, creates deficiency, lack and an inferior quality of life.

There is that scattereth, and yet increaseth; and there is that withholdeth more than is meet, but it tendeth to poverty.

—PROVERBS 11:24

Poverty and shame shall be to him that refuseth instruction: but he that regardeth reproof shall be honoured.

—PROVERBS 13:18

Will man rob God? Yet ye have robbed me. But ye say, Wherein have we robbed thee? In tithes and offerings. Ye are cursed with a curse: for ye have robbed me, even this whole nation. Bring ye all the tithes into the storehouse, that there may be meat in mine house, and prove me now herewith, saith the LORD of hosts, if I will not open you the windows of heaven, and pour you out a blessing, that there shall not be room enough to receive it. And I will rebuke the devourer for your sakes, and he shall not destroy the fruits of your ground; neither shall your vine cast her fruit before the time in the field, saith the LORD of hosts. And all nations shall call you blessed: for ye shall be a delightsome land, saith the LORD of hosts.

—MALACHI 3:8–12

And there was a great cry of the people and of their wives against their brethren the Jews. For there were that said, We, our sons, and our daughters, are many: therefore we take up corn for them, that we may eat, and live. Some also there were that said, We have mortgaged our lands, vineyards, and houses, that we might buy corn, because of the dearth. There were also that said, We have borrowed money for the king's tribute, and that upon our lands and vineyards. Yet now our flesh is as the flesh of our brethren, our children as their children: and, lo, we bring into bondage our sons and our daughters to be servants, and some of our daughters are brought into bondage already: neither is it in our power to redeem them; for other men have our lands and vineyards. And I was very angry when I heard their cry and these words. Then I consulted with myself, and I rebuked the nobles, and the rulers, and said unto them, Ye exact usury, every one of his brother. And I set a great assembly against them. And I said unto them, We after our ability have redeemed our brethren the Jews, which were sold unto the heathen; and will ye even sell your brethren? or shall they be sold unto us? Then held they their peace, and found nothing to answer. Also I said, It is not good that ye do: ought ye not to walk in the fear of our God because of the reproach of the heathen our enemies? Likewise, and my brethren, and my servants, might exact of them money and corn: I pray you, let us leave off this usury. Restore, I pray you, to them, even this day, their lands, their vineyards, their oliveyards, and their houses, also the hundredth part of the money, and of the corn, the wine, and the oil, that ye exact of them.

—NEHEMIAH 5:1–11

| Signs, Symptoms, and Manifestations of the Spirit of Poverty and Financial Curses | | |
|---|---|---|
| Nontithing | Begrudging giving | Extravagance |
| Living above means | Greed | Impropriety |
| Famine | Privation | Indigence |
| Stinginess | Oppression | Debt |
| Hoarding | Defraud | Fear of lack |
| Pestilence | Selfishness | Judgment |
| Gambling | Ingratitude | Ignorance |
| Drug-trafficking | Embezzlement | Deprivation |
| Destitution | Lack | Ignorance |
| Financial curse | Depression | Sickness |
| Shortage | Dearth | Fraud |

| Defect | Want | Pauperism |
|--------|------|-----------|
| Hardship | Addiction | Pride |
| Shame | Waste | Laziness |
| Apathy | Inability to make or keep money | |

**Release:** Prosperity, liberality in giving, faith, truth, and abundance.

# Spirit of Pride

PRIDE IS THE very foundation upon which Satan has built his kingdom. This spirit's origin finds its way into the very heart of Satan. In a way it can be said that Satan himself spawned this spirit. Pride is an inflated perception of one's own dignity and self-worth. When pride manifests itself, it often manifests as arrogance, disdainful conduct or treatment, haughtiness, or even false humility. Pride is a protector of "self." It does not betray or expose self. It is obsessed with self.

> Pride goeth before destruction, and a haughty spirit before a fall.
>
> —PROVERBS 16:18

> Thou hast been in Eden the garden of God; every precious stone was thy covering, the sardius, topaz, and the diamond, the beryl, the onyx, and the jasper, the sapphire, the emerald, and the carbuncle, and gold: the workmanship of thy tabrets and of thy pipes was prepared in thee in the day that thou wast

created. Thou art the anointed cherub that covereth; and I have set thee so: thou wast upon the holy mountain of God; thou hast walked up and down in the midst of the stones of fire. Thou wast perfect in thy ways from the day that thou wast created, till iniquity was found in thee. By the multitude of thy merchandise they have filled the midst of thee with violence, and thou hast sinned: therefore I will cast thee as profane out of the mountain of God: and I will destroy thee, O covering cherub, from the midst of the stones of fire. Thine heart was lifted up because of thy beauty, thou hast corrupted thy wisdom by reason of thy brightness: I will cast thee to the ground, I will lay thee before kings, that they may behold thee. Thou hast defiled thy sanctuaries by the multitude of thine iniquities, by the iniquity of thy traffick; therefore will I bring forth a fire from the midst of thee, it shall devour thee, and I will bring thee to ashes upon the earth in the sight of all them that behold thee. All they that know thee among the people shall be astonished at thee: thou shalt be terror, and never shalt thou be any more.

—EZEKIEL 28:13–19

| Signs, Symptoms, and Manifestations of the Spirit of Pride | | |
|---|---|---|
| Haughtiness | Self-centeredness | Self-importance |
| Selfishness | Self-righteousness | Independence |
| Segregation | Wrath | Separatism |
| Rebellion | Obstinacy | Self-protection |

| Insubordination | Defensiveness | Vanity |
|---|---|---|
| Strife | Conceit | Loftiness |
| Arrogance | Waywardness | Crooked |
| Perverse | Disobedience | Disrespect |
| Disregard of authority | Uncontrolled anger | Bitterness |
| Malice | Hatred | Resentment |
| Jealousy | Guile | Profanity |
| Over-familiarity | Witchcraft | False humility |
| Insolence | Strong delusion | Unteachable spirit |
| Passive aggressive | Deception (all forms) | Perverted mind-set |
| Perverted imagination | Corrupt mind | Stinginess |
| Hoarding | Bondage | Poverty |
| Egotism | Possessiveness | Dominance |
| Control | Withholding self | Self-absorbed |
| Self-promotion (often at another's expense) | | |

**Release:** True humility, submission, repentance, a spirit of giving, and faith.

# Spirit of Rebellion

WORKING WELL WITH the spirit of pride, this spirit resists government and authority in all forms. It drives its hosts to blatantly disobey. It is noncompliant to protocol or order. This spirit creates a disposition that defies authority to the point of insurrection.

> For rebellion is as the sin of witchcraft, and stubbornness is as iniquity and idolatry. Because thou hast rejected the word of the LORD, he hath also rejected thee from being king.
>
> —1 SAMUEL 15:23

> For I know thy rebellion, and thy stiff neck: behold, while I am yet alive with you this day, ye have been rebellious against the LORD; and how much more after my death?
>
> —DEUTERONOMY 31:27

## Signs, Symptoms, and Manifestations of the Spirit of Rebellion

| | | |
|---|---|---|
| Haughtiness | Self-centeredness | Self-importance |
| Selfishness | Self-righteousness | Independence |
| Segregation | Wrath | Separatism |
| Rebellion | Obstinacy | Self-protection |
| Insubordination | Defensiveness | Vanity |
| Strife | Conceit | Loftiness |
| Noncompliance | Defiance | Contempt |
| Recalcitrance | Unruliness | Disobedience |
| Arrogance | Resistance | Waywardness |
| Pride | Rejection of authority | Disdain |
| Scorn | Recalcitrance | |

**Release:** Humility, submission, repentance, and love of God, and compliance.

# Spirit of Rejection

REJECTION IS THE refusal of accepting a person or a thing. This spirit drives people to refuse to accept, recognize, give affection to, submit, believe, make use of, and to socially or politically ostracize another person after examination. The person that rejects usually has a standard by which he or she measures a thing or a person. When they perceive that the person or thing does not measure up to a particular standard or meet a particular criterion, they reject the thing or person. It could be as simple as a type of food or as complicated as wanting to have a boy baby and ending up birthing a girl, or an untimely or unplanned pregnancy, or liking a person, but hating certain things about his or her personality. This is one spirit I believe most people have been attacked by. Depending on your response, rejection can take the wind out of your sail and cause you to drift aimlessly through life without the knowledge of your true worth and dignity.

And Samuel said unto Saul, I will not return with thee: for thou hast rejected the word of the LORD, and the LORD hath rejected thee from being king over Israel....And the LORD said unto Samuel, How long wilt thou mourn for Saul, seeing I have rejected him from reigning over Israel? fill thine horn with oil, and go, I will send thee to Jesse the Beth-lehemite: for I have provided me a king among his sons....But the Spirit of the LORD departed from Saul, and an evil spirit from the LORD troubled him. And Saul's servants said unto him, Behold now, an evil spirit from God troubleth thee. Let our Lord now command thy servants, which are before thee, to seek out a man, who is a cunning player on an harp: and it shall come to pass, when the evil spirit from God is upon thee, that he shall play with his hand, and thou shalt be well. And Saul said unto his servants, Provide me now a man that can play well, and bring him to me. Then answered one of the servants, and said, Behold, I have seen a son of Jesse the Beth-lehemite, that is cunning in playing, and a mighty valiant man, and a man of war, and prudent in matters, and is a comely person, and the LORD is with him. Wherefore Saul sent messengers unto Jesse, and said, Send me David thy son, which is with the sheep. And Jesse took an ass laden with bread, and a bottle of wine, and a kid, and sent them by David his son unto Saul. And David came to Saul, and stood before him: and he loved him greatly; and he loved him greatly; and he became his Armorbearer. And Saul sent to Jesse, saying, Let David, I pray thee, stand before me, for he hath found favor in my sight. And it came to pass, when the evil spirit from God was upon Saul, that David took an harp, and played with his hand: so Saul was refreshed, and was well, and the evil spirit was departed from him....And Saul was very wroth, and the saying displeased him; and he said, They have ascribed unto David ten thousands, and to me they have ascribed but thousands: and what can he have more but the kingdom? And Saul eyed David from that day and foreward. And it came to pass on the morrow, that the evil spirit from God came upon Saul, and he prophesied in the midst of the house: and David played with his hand, as at other times: and there was a javelin in Saul's hand. And Saul cast the javelin; for he said, I will smite David even to the wall with it. And David avoided out of his presence twice. And Saul was afraid of David, because the LORD was with him, and was departed from Saul. Therefore Saul removed him from him, and made him his captain over a thousand; and he went out and came in before the people. And David behaved himself wisely in all his ways; and the Lord was with him. Wherefore when Saul saw that he behaved himself very wisely, he was afraid of him.

—1 SAMUEL 15:26; 16:1, 14–23; 18:8–15

| Signs, Symptoms, and Manifestations of the Spirit of Rejection | | |
|---|---|---|
| Passive-aggressive behavior | Lack of confidence | Repression |
| Fear of (further rejection) | Codependency* | Ignominy |
| Disappointment and guilt | Antisocial disorder | Vexation |

| | | |
|---|---|---|
| Introversion | Inhibition | Lashing out |
| Abuse (of self and others) | Dysfunction | Projection |
| Addictions | Sex for love | Depression |
| Emotional instability | Anger | Bitterness |
| Intense emotional pain | Shame | Anxiety |
| Over-compensation | Negativism | Dejection |
| Sadness/crying | Workaholism | Eating disorder |
| Over-sensitivity | Fear of being alone | Hysteria |
| Distrust | Mistrust | Humiliation |
| Schizophrenia | Self-depreciation | Grief |
| Over-protection | Overweight | Oppression |
| Suicide | Isolation | Betrayal |
| Torment | Emotional trauma | Feelings of rejection |
| Phobia | Loneliness | Emptiness |
| Neurosis | Grandiosity | Abandonment |
| Social isolation | Emotional victimization | Deception |
| Self-consciousness | Psychological victimization | Denial |
| Hopelessness | Emotional callousness | Murder |
| Bashfulness | Disrepute | Disesteem |
| Discredit | Worthlessness | Insignificance |
| Disgrace | Need for approval/validation | Dishonor |
| Suspicions | Segregation | Exile |

| Eviction | Scorn | Shun |
|---|---|---|
| Ignore/neglect | Insecurities | Low self-worth |
| Disapproval | Repudiation | Comparison |
| Favoritism | Emotional/ psychological rape | Self-fulfilling prophecy |
| False/ nonexpectations | Post-traumatic stress disorder | Dysfunctions |
| Perversions | Feelings of not being wanted | "Nobody loves me" syndrome (self-pity) |
| Inability to receive/ give love | Justification of inappropriate word/behavior | Sabotage (relation- ships/organization/ self/purpose/ destinies) |

**Release:** Love, the mind of Christ, restoration, healing, deliverance, faith, hope, and forgiveness.

And all things, whatsoever ye shall ask in prayer, believing, ye shall receive.

—Matthew 21:22

# Spirit of Religion

A SPIRIT OF RELIGION portrays itself as having a very high devotion to God or a deity, but merely deceives its hosts into placing more emphasis on religious activities than a true relationship with God. In the trial of Jesus, we see another spirit called the spirit of Barabas, which seeks to make scapegoats of others. It is a spirit that assassinates and maligns.

> For ye have heard of my conversation in time past in the Jews' religion, how that beyond measure I persecuted the church of God, and wasted it: And profited in the Jews' religion above many my equals in mine own nation, being more exceedingly zealous of the traditions of my fathers.
>
> —GALATIANS 1:13–14

> Ye fools and blind: for whether is greater, the gold, or the temple that sanctifieth the gold?
>
> —MATTHEW 23:17

> Now the Spirit speaketh expressly, that in the latter

times some shall depart from the faith, giving heed to seducing spirits, and doctrines of devils; Speaking lies in hypocrisy; having their conscience seared with a hot iron.

—1 TIMOTHY 4:1–2

And as he spake, a certain Pharisee besought him to dine with him: and he went in, and sat down to meat. And when the Pharisee saw it, he marvelled that he had not first washed before dinner. And the Lord said unto him, now do ye Pharisees make clean the outside of the cup and the platter; but your inward part is full of ravening and wickedness. Ye fools, did not he that made that which is without make that which is within also? But rather give alms of such things as ye have; and, behold, all things are clean unto you. But woe unto you, Pharisees! for ye tithe mint and rue and all manner of herbs, and pass over judgment and the love of God: these ought ye to have done, and not to leave the other undone. Woe unto you, Pharisees! for ye love the uppermost seats in the synagogues, and greetings in the markets. Woe unto you, scribes and Pharisees, hypocrites! for ye are as graves which appear not, and the men that walk over them are not aware of them. Then answered one of the lawyers, and said unto him, Master, thus saying thou reproachest us also. And he said, Woe unto you also, ye lawyers! for ye lade men with burdens grievous to be borne, and ye yourselves touch not the burdens with one of your fingers. Woe unto you! for ye build the sepulchres of the prophets, and your fathers killed them. Truly ye bear witness that ye allow the deeds of your fathers: for they indeed killed them, and ye build their sepulchres. Therefore also said the wisdom of God, I will send them prophets and apostles, and some of them they shall slay and persecute: That the blood of all the prophets, which was shed from the foundation of the world, may be required of this generation; From the blood of Abel unto the blood of Zecharias, which perished between the altar and the temple: verily I say unto you, It shall be required of this generation. Woe unto you, lawyers! for ye have taken away the key of knowledge: ye entered not in yourselves, and them that were entering in ye hindered. And as he said these things unto them, the scribes and the Pharisees began to urge him vehemently, and to provoke him to speak of many things: Laying wait for him, and seeking to catch something out of his mouth, that they might accuse him.

—LUKE 11:37–54

| Signs, Symptoms, and Manifestations of the Spirit of Religion | | |
|---|---|---|
| Unteachableness | Idolatry | Hypocrisy |
| Pride | Spiritual adultery | Traditionalism |
| Formalism | Inordinate sophistication | Arrogance |
| Ritualism | Nonsubmissiveness | Phariseeism |
| Sadduceeism | Polarity in membership | Unbelief |
| Vain babbling | Negativism | Obstinacy |
| Superstition | "Holier than thou" attitude | Libations |

| Ancestral worship | Occultism | Spiritism |
|---|---|---|
| Voodoo | Treachery | Seduction |
| Doctrines of devils | Deception | Judgmentalism |
| Heresies | Denominationalism | Dogmatism |
| Hireling anointing | Antagonism | Emotionalism |
| Division | Self-righteousness | Fables |
| Disunity | Disharmony | Control |
| Falsehood | Cultism | Duplicity |
| Prosecution of truth | Blasphemy | Unholy |
| Sacrilege | Heresy | Irreverence |
| Institutionalized abuse | "Religiosity" | False apostolic anointing |
| Scapegoating | Spirit of Barabas | Character assassination |
| False revelation | Abortion | False evangelistic anointing |
| False prophetic anointing | False pastoral anointing | False pedagogical (teaching) anointing |

**Release:** The Spirit of Truth, prophetic anointing/ utterance, discerning of spirits, and the spirit of John the Baptist.

**Declare:** The Lamb of God Jesus Christ has been slain even before the foundations of the world. Apply the blood to the doorposts of your soul.

# Spirit of Sabotage

THE SPIRIT OF sabotage operates as strong demonic influences that drive people to abort the progress and success of divinely ordained projects, purposes relationships, organization, self, potential, and destinies. It stirs up jealousy, resentment, and suspicion, and is often vindictive toward the person who detects its presence. Sabotage can make you both victim and perpetrator so that even when you pronounce judgment on others you both expose and pronounce judgment upon yourself. This spirit is so skillful it will use you as a pawn and a puppet on a string, prohibiting you from detecting its hand upon you and the strings that manipulate you. Working with familiar spirits, who act as their reconnaissance, informing them of breaks in hedges of protection, strengths, weaknesses, and proclivities of both the perpetrator and victim, its plan is a well-thought-out plan. I have discovered that many agents used are not only those with malicious intent, but also those who sincerely love us and want what's best for us. Consider the incident Matthew records in Matthew 16:21–23, where Peter unwittingly was being used in an attempt to sabotage the mission of Jesus. Jesus decisively identified the spirit controlling Peter's thoughts and immediately aborted its activities. Remember as you examine the activities of this spirit that you will discover that you are both victim and perpetrator. When the Lord gives you victory over this spirit, you will notice that a veil will be lifted, and scales of deception will fall from your spiritual eyes. Everything that you thought was real will crumbles before you and evaporates like a mirage. Truth will prevail and set you free from anything built upon fabrications, lies, falsehood, and untruths.

Nehemiah had the ability to recognize this spirit and anyone remotely associated with those who operated by it he drove them away. Nehemiah 13:28 states, "And one of the sons of Joiada, the son of Eliashib the high priest, was son in law to Sanballat the Horonite: therefore I chased him from me." I pray that the eyes of your understanding will be enlightened as you study the characteristics of this power demonic force and that God will empower you to drive this spirit away.

> When Sanballat the Horonite, and Tobiah the ser-
> vant, the Ammonite, heard of it, it grieved them
> exceedingly that there was come a man to seek the
> welfare of the children of Israel…Then said I unto
> them, Ye see the distress that we are in, how Jeru-
> salem lieth waste, and the gates thereof are burned
> with fire: come, and let us build up the wall of Jeru-
> salem, that we be no more a reproach. Then I told
> them of the hand of my God which was good upon
> me; as also the king's words that he had spoken unto
> me. And they said, Let us rise up and build. So they

strengthened their hands for this good work. But when Sanballat the Horonite, and Tobiah the servant, the Ammonite, and Geshem the Arabian, heard it, they laughed us to scorn, and despised us, and said, what is this thing that ye do? will ye rebel against the king? Then answered I them, and said unto them, the God of heaven, he will prosper us; therefore we his servants will arise and build: but ye have no portion, nor right, nor memorial, in Jerusalem.

—NEHEMIAH 2:10, 17–20

But it came to pass, that when Sanballat heard that we builded the wall, he was wroth, and took great indignation, and mocked the Jews....But it came to pass, that when Sanballat, and Tobiah, and the Arabians, and the Ammonites, and the Ashdodites, heard that the walls of Jerusalem were made up, and that the breaches began to be stopped, then they were very wroth.

—NEHEMIAH 4:1, 7

Now it came to pass, when Sanballat, and Tobiah, and Geshem the Arabian, and the rest of our enemies, heard that I had builded the wall, and that there was no breach left therein; (though at that time I had not set up the doors upon the gates;) That Sanballat and Geshem sent unto me, saying, come, let us meet together in some one of the villages in the plain of Ono. But they thought to do me mischief. And I sent messengers unto them, saying, I am doing a great work, so that I cannot come down: why should the work cease, whilst I leave it, and come down to you? Yet they sent unto me four times after this sort; and I answered them after the same manner. Then sent Sanballat his servant unto me in like manner the fifth time with an open letter in his hand; Wherein was written, It is reported among the heathen, and Gashmu saith it, that thou and the Jews think to rebel: for which cause thou buildest the wall, that thou mayest be their king, according to these words. And thou hast also appointed prophets to preach of thee at Jerusalem, saying, There is a king in Judah: and now shall it be reported to the king according to these words. Come now therefore, and let us take counsel together. Then I sent unto him, saying, There are no such things done as thou sayest, but thou feignest them out of thine own heart. For they all made us afraid, saying, Their hands shall be weakened from the work, that it be not done. Now therefore, O God, strengthen my hands. Afterward I came unto the house of Shemaiah the son of Delaiah the son of Mehetabeel, who was shut up; and he said, Let us meet together in the house of God, within the temple, and let us shut the doors of the temple: for they will come to slay thee; yea, in the night will they come to slay thee. And I said, Should such a man as I flee? and who is there, that, being as I am, would go into the temple to save his life? I will not go in. And, lo, I perceived that God had not sent him; but that he pronounced this prophecy against me: for Tobiah and Sanballat had hired him. Therefore was he hired, that I should be afraid, and do so, and sin, and that they might have matter for an evil report, that they might reproach me. My God, think thou upon Tobiah and Sanballat according to these their works, and on the prophetess Noadiah, and the rest of the prophets, that would have put me in fear.

—NEHEMIAH 6:1–14

Hear, O our God; for we are despised: and turn their reproach upon their own head, and give them for a prey in the land of captivity: And cover not their iniquity, and let not their sin be blotted out from before thee: for they have provoked thee to anger before the builder. So built we the wall; and all the wall was joined together unto the half thereof: for the people had a mind to work.... Nevertheless we made our prayer unto our God, and set a watch against them day and night, because of them.... Therefore set I in the lower places behind the wall, and on the higher places, I even set the people after their families with their swords, their spears, and their bows. And I looked, and rose up, and said unto the nobles, and to the rulers, and to the rest of the people, Be not ye afraid of them: remember the Lord, which is great and terrible, and fight for your brethren, your sons, and your daughters, your wives, and your houses.

—NEHEMIAH 4:4–6, 9, 13–14

## Signs, Symptoms, and Manifestations of the Spirit of Sabotage

| | | |
|---|---|---|
| Discouragement | Ulterior motives | Spirit of scorn |
| Disbelief | Derailment | Indignation |
| Mockery | Faithlessness | Ridicule |
| Conspiracy | Religiosity | Subversion |

| Threatening | Opposition | Unholy alliances |
|---|---|---|
| Suspicion | Deception | Falsehood |
| Slander | Isolation | Manipulation |
| Passive-aggressive | Gossip | Treacheries |
| "Cutthroat" activities | Betrayal | Jealousy |
| Abortive activities | Abandonment | Accusations |
| Covert behavior | Superficiality | Disloyalty |
| Rationalization | Spiritual blindness | Anxiety |
| Seduction | Vexation | Backlash |
| Mental affliction | Pride | Traditions of men |
| Religious spirits | Murder | Embezzlement |
| Desolation | Withholding | Fear |
| Irrational thinking | Rejection | Emotional seduction |
| Psychological games | Diabolical traps | Schemes |
| Snares | Victimization | Demoralization |
| Frustration | Recrimination | Threats |
| Castigation | Ultimatums | Envy |
| Prejudice | Hatred | Strife |
| Competition | Blaspheme | Disrespect of authority |
| Malicious destruction | Disruption | Corruption |
| Violence | Condemnation | Belligerence |
| Rebellion | Insurrection | Double-mindedness |
| Justification | Antichrist spirit | Judgementalism |
| Forgetfulness | Censorship | Surveillance |

| Confusion | Disenfranchisement | Desertion |
|---|---|---|
| Grandiosity | Selfishness | Rivalry |
| Witchcraft | Criticism | Fault-finding |
| Fabrication | Disapproval | Disassociation |
| Resentment | Unconfessed sins | Lack of accountability |
| Carnality | Leanness of the soul | Hypocrisy |
| Family secrets | Adultery | Fornication |
| Perversion | Underhandedness | Rumors |
| Pilfering | Doctrine of devils | Attachment |
| Ignorance | Indifference | Dishonor |
| Shame | Iniquity | Arrogance |
| Revengefulness | Unforgiveness | Identity theft |
| Suppressed emotions | Projections | Secretiveness |
| Self-centeredness | Stigmatization | Bad reputation |
| Church splits | Irreverence | Difficult personality |
| Impudence | Fraudulence | Vulgarity |
| Disrespect | Harassment | Stinginess |
| Noncompliance | Obstinacy | Impudence |
| Cruelty | Harshness | Hard-heartedness |
| Lethargy | Stubbornness | Sorrowful |
| Abuse | Severity | Self-sabotage |
| Grief | Surreptitious activities | Alienation |
| Allegation | False prophecies | Incrimination |
| Self-doubt | Character assassination | Trouble-making |

| Offences | Helplessness | Scandal |
|---|---|---|
| Loss | Compromizing | Weariness |
| Fatigue | Loss of motivation | Loss of focus |
| Silence/silent treatment | Guilt-tripping | Lack of trust |
| Evil | Addiction | Oppression |
| Undermining trust | Stealing | Sanballat and Tobiah |
| Poor nutritional habit | Greed | Gluttony |
| Fatigue | Death | Knowledge block |
| Feelings of incompetence | Misrepresentation of truth | Undermining activities/cause |
| Erosion of self-worth and image | Ineffective decision-making | Bad habits (eating, social, spending, etc.) |
| Plotting and planning the demise of institutions/people | Creating wedges in relationships | Undermining and destroying covenant relationships |

**Release:** Prayer, fasting, intercession, *Jehovah Gibbor*, the Spirit of Truth, discernment of spirits, repentance, the wisdom of God, revelation of the hidden secrets of the heart.

# Spirit of Samaria

ACCORDING TO THE prophet Ezekiel, Samaria was known for its spiritual harlotry and adultery in that it promoted convenience in worship, compromise of holiness and mediocrity in the service of the Lord, which eventually led the children of Israel to embrace carnality, sensuality, and idolatry as a way of life, possessing a form of godliness, but denying the power therein.

The word of the LORD came again unto me, saying, Son of man, there were two women, the daughters of one mother: And they committed whoredoms in Egypt; they committed whoredoms in their youth: there were their breasts pressed, and there they bruised the teats of their virginity. And the names of them were Aholah the elder, and Aholibah her sister: and they were mine, and they bare sons and daughters. Thus were their names; Samaria is Aholah, and Jerusalem Aholibah. And Aholah played the harlot when she was mine; and she doted on her lovers, on the Assyrians her neighbours, Which were clothed with blue, captains and rulers, all of them desirable young men, horsemen riding upon horses. Thus she committed her whoredoms with them, with all them that were the chosen men of Assyria, and with all on whom she doted: with all their idols she defiled herself. Neither left she her whoredoms brought from Egypt: for in her youth they lay with her, and they bruised the breasts of her virginity, and poured their whoredom upon her. Wherefore I have delivered her into the hand of her lovers, into the hand of the Assyrians, upon whom she doted. These discovered her nakedness: they took her sons and her daughters, and slew her with the sword: and she became famous among women; for they had executed judgment upon her. And when her sister Aholibah saw this, she was more corrupt in her inordinate love than she, and in her whoredoms more than her sister in her whoredoms. She doted upon the Assyrians her neighbours, captains and rulers clothed most gorgeously, horsemen riding upon horses, all of them desirable young men. Then I saw that she was defiled, that they took both one way, And that she increased her whoredoms: for when she saw men pourtrayed upon the wall, the images of the Chaldeans pourtrayed with vermilion, Girded with girdles upon their loins, exceeding in dyed attire upon their heads, all of them princes to look to, after the manner of the Babylonians of Chaldea, the land of their nativity: And as soon as she saw them with her eyes, she doted upon them, and sent messengers unto them into Chaldea. And the Babylonians came to her into the bed of love, and they defiled her with their whoredom, and she was polluted with them, and her mind was alienated from them. So she discovered her whoredoms, and discovered her nakedness: then my mind was alienated from her, like as my mind was alienated from her sister. Yet she multiplied her whoredoms, in calling to remembrance the days of her youth, wherein she had played the harlot in the land of Egypt. For she doted upon their paramours, whose flesh is as the flesh of asses, and whose issue is like the issue of horses.

—EZEKIEL 23:1–20

## Signs, Symptoms, and Manifestations of the Spirit of Samaria

| | | |
|---|---|---|
| Idolatry | Spiritual harlotry | Lust |
| Fornication | Witchcraft/sorcery | Perversion |
| Religious spirit | Formalism | Dogmatism |
| Unteachableness | Hypocrisy | Pride |
| Spiritual adultery | Traditionalism | Inordinate sophistication |
| Arrogance | Ritualism | Nonsubmissiveness |
| Phariseeism | Sadduceeism | Polarity in membership |
| Unbelief | Vain babbling | Negativism |
| Obstinacy | Superstition | "Holier than thou" attitude |
| Libations | Ancestral worship | Occultism |
| Spiritism | Voodoo | Treachery |
| Seduction | Doctrines of devils | Judgmentalism |
| Deception | Heresies | Denominationalism |

| Hireling anointing | Antagonism | Emotionalism |
|---|---|---|
| Division | Self-righteousness | Fables |
| Disunity | Disharmony | Control |
| Falsehood | Cultism | Duplicity |
| Prosecution of truth | Blasphemy | Unholy |
| Sacrilege | Heresy | Irreverence |
| Institutionalized abuse | "Religiosity" | Compromise |
| Worldliness | Unrighteousness | Lewdness |
| Rebellion | Idolatry | False apostolic anointing |
| Scapegoating | Spirit of Barabas | Character assassination |
| False revelation | Abortion | False evangelistic anointing |
| Carnality | Traditions of man | False prophetic anointing |
| False pastoral anointing | Whoredom | False pedagogical (teaching) anointing |

**Release:** *Jehovah Gibbor*, Holiness, and the Spirit of Truth.

# Seducing Spirit

THE SEDUCING SPIRIT opens the gates of the soul of man, cities, and nations (natural and spiritual) to the spirit of perversion. It is a counterfeit of the anointing and an imitator of the Holy Spirit. It forms a strong confederation with a religious spirit and is fueled by the spirit of the Antichrist.

> But king Solomon loved many strange women, together with the daughter of Pharaoh, women of the Moabites, Ammonites, Edomites, Zidonians, and Hittites; Of the nations concerning which the LORD said unto the children of Israel, Ye shall not go in to them, neither shall they come in unto you: for surely they will turn away your heart after their gods: Solomon clave unto these in love. And he had seven hundred wives, princesses, and three hundred concubines: and his wives turned away his heart. For it came to pass, when Solomon was old, that his wives turned away his heart after other gods: and his heart was not perfect with the LORD his God, as

was the heart of David his father. For Solomon went after Ashtoreth the goddess of the Zidonians, and after Milcom the abomination of the Ammonites. And Solomon did evil in the sight of the LORD, and went not fully after the LORD, as did David his father. Then did Solomon build an high place for Chemosh, the abomination of Moab, in the hill that is before Jerusalem, and for Molech, the abomination of the children of Ammon. And likewise did he for all his strange wives, which burnt incense and sacrificed unto their gods.

—1 KINGS 11:1–8

Now the Spirit speaketh expressly, that in the latter times some shall depart from the faith, giving heed to seducing spirits, and doctrines of devils; Speaking lies in hypocrisy; having their conscience seared with a hot iron; Forbidding to marry, and commanding to abstain from meats, which God hath created to be received with thanksgiving of them which believe and know the truth. For every creature of God is good, and nothing to be refused, if it be received with thanksgiving: For it is sanctified by the word of God and prayer. If thou put the brethren in remembrance of these things, thou shalt be a good minister of Jesus Christ, nourished up in the words of faith and of good doctrine, whereunto thou hast attained.

—1 TIMOTHY 4:1–6

Notwithstanding I have a few things against thee, because thou sufferest that woman Jezebel, which calleth herself a prophetess, to teach and to seduce my servants to commit fornication, and to eat things sacrificed unto idols. And I gave her space to repent of her fornication; and she repented not. Behold, I will cast her into a bed, and them that commit adultery with her into great tribulation, except they repent of their deeds. And I will kill her children with death; and all the churches shall know that I am he which searcheth the reins and hearts: and I will give unto every one of you according to your works.

—REVELATION 2:20–23

## Signs, Symptoms, and Manifestations of Seducing Spirits

| | | |
|---|---|---|
| Subtlety | Carnality | Sensuality |
| Humanism | Iniquitous | Witchcraft |
| Renegades | Deception | Charmers |
| Divination | Lying | Spiritual adultery |
| Spiritual idolatry | Astrology | Psychics |
| Prognosticators | Enchanters | Miracle workers |
| Witches | Warlocks | Idolatry |
| Fornication | False teaching | False prophets |
| False religion | Homosexuality | Flattery |
| Doctrines of devils | Perversion | Spirit of Jezebel |
| Hypocrisy | Satanic stupor | False teachers |
| False prophets | False apostles | |

**Release:** The anointing of the Holy Spirit, gifts of the Spirit, discerning spirits, Spirit of truth, the wrath of God (see Ezekiel 13:11–15), and the prophetic anointing.

# Spirit of Shame

THIS SPIRIT CAUSES shame-based societies, homes, and families. It causes painful emotions, a strong sense of guilt, embarrassment, unworthiness, and disgrace. Many people grow up in shame-based homes and communities. Individuals who are plagued by the spirit of shame walk through life like emotional puppets. They are easily manipulated and often use manipulation to get people to do what they want. The also walk around with feelings of unworthiness, poor self-image, and self-worth. Unconditional love, positive regard, and deep inner healing are needed for anyone plagued by this spirit. Read 2 Samuel 13 for greater understanding of shame.

> Because for thy sake I have borne reproach; shame hath covered my face.
>
> —PSALM 69:7

## Signs, Symptoms, and Manifestations of the Spirit of Shame

| | | |
|---|---|---|
| Guilt | Humiliation | Flawed view of self |
| Embarrassment | Hypersensitivity | Dysfunction |
| Hopelessness | Helplessness | Sadness |
| Abuse | Perfectionism | Blame |
| Phobias | Enmeshment | Fear |
| Emotional deprivation | Paranoid personality | Sexual addictions |
| Substance abuse | Gambling | Poverty |
| Pornography | Instability | Control |
| Projections | Perversion | Physical abuse |
| Nightmares | Impaired will | Incest |
| Molestation | Unholy alliance | Repetition compulsion |
| Reenactments | Victimization | Hypochondria |
| Pseudo-intimacy | Spirits of inheritance | Confusion |
| Psychological pain | Mental anguish | Stigmatization |
| Ostracization | Boundary violation | Fetish behavior |
| Sodomy | Heaviness | Grief |
| Apathy | Exasperation | Distress |
| Isolation | Self-loathing | Immaturity |
| Shame-based relationships | Shame-based homes | Suspicion |
| Shame-based societies | Dishonor | Competition |

| Mourning | Abandonment | Codependence |
|---|---|---|
| Psychosomatic illness | Prostitution | Homosexuality |
| Post-traumatic stress disorder | Gossip | Fornication |
| External locus of control | Ignominy | Oversensitivity |
| Excessive self-analysis | Faulty perspectives | Lust |
| Little boy/girl syndrome | Impropriety | Overcompensation |
| Loss of perception | Intimidation | Loneliness |
| Insignificance | Violence | Mutilation |
| Lack of connectedness | False humility | Knowledge block |
| Effeminacy | Erosion of self-esteem | Rejection |
| Enslavement of emotions | | |

**Release:** Healing, deliverance, faith, integrity, restoration, hope, and the fruit of the Spirit.

# Spirit of Suspicion

THIS SPIRIT SEDUCES people into forming judgments and arriving at conclusions based on what appears to be factual. It is a spirit that creates insecurities, division, and strong mistrust. Due to its nature it often works at creating and sustaining disunity.

And Saul was very wroth, and the saying displeased him; and he said, They have ascribed unto David ten thousands, and to me they have ascribed but thousands: and what can he have more but the kingdom? And Saul eyed David from that day and forward. And it came to pass on the morrow, that the evil spirit from God came upon Saul, and he prophesied in the midst of the house: and David played with his hand, as at other times: and there was a javelin in Saul's hand. And Saul cast the javelin; for he said, I will smite David even to the wall with it. And David avoided out of his presence twice. And Saul was afraid of David, because the LORD was with him, and was departed from Saul. Therefore

Saul removed him from him, and made him his captain over a thousand; and he went out and came in before the people. And David behaved himself wisely in all his ways; and the LORD was with him. Wherefore when Saul saw that he behaved himself very wisely, he was afraid of him.

—1 SAMUEL 18:8–15

| Signs, Symptoms, and Manifestations of the Spirit of Seduction | | |
| --- | --- | --- |
| Doubt | Alienation | Discord |
| Judgementalism | Criticism | Gossip |
| Skepticism | Mistrust | Paranoia |
| Imagination | Speculation | Assumption |
| Presumption | Anxiety | Apprehension |
| Lack of trust | Isolation | Disunity |
| Misjudgment | Misunderstanding | Prejudice |

**Release:** Faith, honesty, integrity, restoration, and harmony.

# Spirit of Tradition

THIS SPIRIT IS responsible for the passing down of elements of a culture, philosophies, behaviors, and habits from generation to generation. This spirit works with religious spirit and the spirit of unbelief. It forms a stronghold that facilitates the rejection of truth, thus hindering true worship and revival. This spirit is a powerful gatekeeper that prohibits the preaching of the gospel within a particular culture, region, or nation, and initiates and instigates both the persecution and martyrdom of any child of God who dares to venture into its jurisdiction with the gospel.

> For laying aside the commandment of God, ye hold the tradition of men, as the washing of pots and cups: and many other such like things ye do.
>
> —MARK 7:8

> Beware lest any man spoil you through philosophy and vain deceit, after the tradition of men, after the rudiments of the world, and not after Christ.
>
> —COLOSSIANS 2:8

## Signs, Symptoms, and Manifestations of the Spirit of Tradition

| | | |
|---|---|---|
| Contention | Intellectualism | Arguments |
| Rationalization | Pride | Legalism |
| Denominationalism | Separatism | Condemnation |
| High things | Doctrines of man | Heresy |
| Superstitions | Unbelief | Strongholds |
| Persecution | Martyrdom | Religious spirit |
| Doctrines of devils | Harassment | Resistance to truth |
| Bondage | Anti-Semitism | Unteachableness |
| Idolatry | Hypocrisy | Spiritual adultery |
| Traditionalism | Formalism | Inordinate sophistication |
| Arrogance | Ritualism | Nonsubmissiveness |
| Phariseeism | Sadduceeism | Polarity in membership |
| Vain babbling | Negativism | Obstinacy |
| Superstition | "Holier than thou" attitude | Libations |
| Ancestral worship | Occultism | Spiritism |
| Voodoo | Treachery | Seduction |
| Judgmentalism | Deception | Heresies |
| Denominationalism | Dogmatism | Hireling anointing |
| Antagonism | Emotionalism | Division |
| Self-righteousness | Fables | Disunity |
| Disharmony | Control | Falsehood |
| Cultism | Duplicity | Prosecution of truth |

| Blasphemy | Unholy alliances | Sacrilege |
|---|---|---|
| Secret sects | Irreverence | Institutionalized abuse |
| "Religiosity" | False apostolic anointing | Scapegoating |
| Spirit of Barabas | Character assassination | False revelation |
| Abortion | Resistance to moves of God | False evangelistic anointing |
| False prophetic anointing | False pastoral anointing | False pedagogical (teaching) anointing |

**Release:** Revival, visitation of God, apostolic, prophetic anointing, and the spirit of truth.

# Unclean Spirits

ACCORDING TO REVELATION 16:13, this spirit has a frog-like characteristic and is directly associated with idolatry, witchcraft, and vileness. This spirit works in confederation with many other spirits and is often a doorkeeper in the lives of individuals and a gatekeeper in nations, cities, and communities, such as biblical Sodom and Gomorrah. An unclean spirit entangles itself with the very essence of the person that it possesses. It is a spirit that is not always easy to identify because of its intent to seduce, influence, and eventually possess an individual. However, if you carefully listen to the contents of the host's conversations, or watch the lifestyle of the host, this spirit will eventually reveal itself, for example, through sexual innuendoes, lewd conversations, dress codes, behaviors, and filthy environment. James 3:11–12 states: "Doth a fountain send forth at the same place sweet water and bitter? Can the fig tree, my brethren, bear olive berries? either a vine, figs? so can no fountain both yield salt water and fresh."

First Corinthians 10:21 states that "Ye cannot drink the cup of the Lord, and the cup of devils: ye cannot be partakers of the Lord's table, and of the table of devils." This spirit undermines potential, taints and contaminates the anointing, displaces individuals, and dispossesses them of both their spiritual and natural rights. In my research, I discovered that many people in the Bible who were possessed by an unclean spirit suffered from convulsions. This spirit has the power of a total ruination of a person's life because it attacks the mind, body, and spirit, corroding the foundation of moral and ethical living. Because of the nature of this spirit, very few people who live a life plagued by this spirit, whether male or female, live out half their life expectancy with a good quality of life. They generally die martyred by their own lusts. According to Mark 1:21–26, the propensities of this spirit is to twist and pervert the very nature of its host, and will be at its most violent and vile state as soon as there is a determination that its victim desires conversion and to serve God.

> And it shall come to pass in that day, saith the Lord of hosts, that I will cut off the names of the idols out of the land, and they shall no more be remembered: and also I will cause the prophets and the unclean spirit to pass out of the land.
>
> —Zechariah 13:2

> When the unclean spirit is gone out of a man, he walketh through dry places, seeking rest, and findeth none.
>
> —Matthew 12:43

And unclean spirits, when they saw him, fell down before him, and cried, saying, Thou art the Son of God.

—MARK 3:11

## Signs, Symptoms, and Manifestations of Unclean Spirits

| | | |
|---|---|---|
| Deception | Divination | Adultery |
| Perversions | Demonic activities | Fornication |
| Lying | Rebellion | Vexation |
| Pretense | Witchcraft | Disease |
| Impure motives | Impure thoughts | Seduction |
| Fantasies | Instability | Vileness |
| Homosexuality | Incest | Soul ties |
| Victimization | Inordinate affections | Manipulation |
| Disloyalty | Carnality | Idolatry |
| Mental afflictions | Immorality | Foulness |
| Tainted anointing | Uncleanness | Traditions of men |
| Antichrist religions | Doctrines of devils | Superstitions |
| Addictions | Physiological bondage | Emotional torment |
| Spirits of inheritance | Sexually explicit dreams | Voyeurism |
| Prostitution | Pornography | Pedophilia |

| Guilt | Humiliation | Flawed view of self |
|---|---|---|
| Embarrassment | Hypersensitivity | Dysfunction |
| Hopelessness | Helplessness | Sadness |
| Abuse | Perfectionism | Blame |
| Phobias | Enmeshment | Fear |
| Emotional deprivation | Paranoid personality | Sexual addictions |
| Substance abuse | Gambling | Poverty |
| Control | Projections | Physical abuse |
| Nightmares | Impaired will | Molestation |
| Unholy alliance | Repetition compulsion | Reenactments |
| Hypochondria | Pseudo-intimacy | Spirits of inheritance |
| Confusion | Psychological pain | Mental anguish |
| Stigmatization | Ostracization | Boundary violation |
| Fetish behavior | Sodomy | Heaviness |
| Grief | Apathy | Exasperation |
| Distress | Isolation | Self-loathing |
| Immaturity | Shame-based relationships | Shame-based homes |
| Suspicion | Shame-based societies | Dishonor |
| Competition | Sexual enslavement | Abandonment |
| Codependence | Psychosomatic illness | Post-traumatic stress disorder |

| | | |
|---|---|---|
| Gossip | External locus of control | Ignominy |
| Oversensitivity | Excessive self-analysis | Faulty perspectives |
| Lust | Sexual enslavement | Irreverence |
| Nonconformity | Antichrist | Lewdness |
| Obscenity | Cultism | Sexual innuendoes |
| Propaganda | Betrayal | Death |
| Disillusionment | Convulsions | Stealing |
| Cheating | Depravity | Oppression |
| Eating disorders | Suicide | Emotional trauma |
| Feelings of rejection | Phobia | Loneliness |
| Emptiness | Neurosis | Grandiosity |
| Social isolation | Emotional victimization | Self-consciousness |
| Psychological victimization | Denial | Emotional callousness |
| Murder | Bashfulness | Disrepute |
| Disesteem | Discredit | Worthlessness |
| Insignificance | Disgrace | Need for approval/ validation |
| Suspicions | False/ nonexpectations | Discrimination |
| Segregation | Exile | Eviction |
| Scorn | Shun | Ignore/Neglect |
| Insecurities | Low self-worth | Disapproval |

| Emotional/ psychological rape | Self-fulfilling prophecy | Leanness of the soul |
| --- | --- | --- |

**Release:** Deliverance, holiness, righteousness, and the fruit of the Spirit.

# Vexation Spirits

THIS SPIRIT CHANGES the quality or condition of lives through constant harassment, annoyance, and irritation. It is especially assigned to those in pursuit of purpose. It creates feelings or exasperation, often driving the victim to give up.

> Now when the adversaries of Judah and Benjamin heard that the children of the captivity builded the temple unto the LORD God of Israel; Then they came to Zerubbabel, and to the chief of the fathers, and said unto them, Let us build with you: for we seek your God, as ye do; and we do sacrifice unto him since the days of Esarhaddon king of Assur, which brought us up hither. But Zerubbabel, and Jeshua, and the rest of the chief of the fathers of Israel, said unto them, Ye have nothing to do with us to build an house unto our God; but we ourselves together will build unto the LORD God of Israel, as king Cyrus the king of Persia hath commanded us. Then the people of the land weakened the hands of

the people of Judah, and troubled them in building, And hired counsellors against them, to frustrate their purpose, all the days of Cyrus king of Persia, even until the reign of Darius king of Persia. And in the reign of Ahaseurus, in the beginning of his reign, wrote they unto him an accusation against the inhabitants of Judah and Jerusalem.

—EZRA 4:1–6

Now about that time Herod the king stretched forth his hands to vex certain of the church.

—ACTS 12:1

Vex the Midianites, and smite them: For they vex you with their wiles, wherewith they have beguiled you in the matter of Peor, and in the matter of Cozbi, the daughter of a prince of Midian, their sister, which was slain in the day of the plague for Peor's sake.

—NUMBERS 25:17–18

But if ye will not drive out the inhabitants of the land from before you; then it shall come to pass, that those which ye let remain of them shall be pricks in your eyes, and thorns in your sides, and shall vex you in the land wherein ye dwell.

—NUMBERS 33:55

## Signs, Symptoms, and Manifestations of Vexation Spirits

| Emotional instability | Discouragement | Distress |
|---|---|---|
| Mental agitation | Paranoia | Stress |

| Antagonism | Frustration | Irritation |
|---|---|---|
| Weariness | Anxiety | Delirium |
| Painful thoughts | Repression | Despondency |
| Undermining purpose | Disgust | Tension |
| Disillusionment | Subversion | Accusation |
| Indecision | Dread | Bitterness |
| Knowledge block | Restlessness | Hyperactivity |
| Worry | Oppression | Distraction |
| Annoyance | Aggravation | Exasperation |
| Victimization | Hounding | Confusion |
| Addiction | Provocation | Hostility |

**Release:** Prophetic anointing, favor of God, discerning of spirits, and a hedge of protection.

Better is an handful with quietness, than both the hands full with travail and vexation of spirit.

—ECCLESIASTES 4:6

# Index

## OTHER MATERIALS
## BY DR. N. CINDY TRIMM

To supplement your prayers and extend your prayer time, these messages are available in tape, CD, book, or bookmark form:

*The Rules of Engagement, Volume I: The Art of Strategic Prayer and Spiritual Warfare*

*The Rules of Engagement, Volume III: Satanic Weapons Esposed*

*The Prayer Journal*

*The Rules of Engagement, Volume IV: The Weapons of Our Warfare*
(scheduled release: 2006)

*The Rules of Engagement, Volume V: The Spirit of the Watchman*

*The Rules of Engagement, Volume VI: Using the Names of God*

*The Rules of Engagement, Volume VII: The Power of the Anointing*
(scheduled release: 2006)

*Who I Am in Christ*

*What I Believe the Lord For*

*The Battle Cry of a Warrior*

*Millennium Creed*

*Names of Jesus*

*Names of the Holy Spirit*

*Prayers for the Saints*

# ABOUT THE AUTHOR

For over twenty-five years this dynamic, multigifted world changer has been equipping people to fulfill their destinies and maximize their potential. Highly respected by persons from all walks of life, a teacher of teachers, preacher, coach, mentor, consultant, author, and former government senator, Dr. N. Cindy Trimm reaches into the depths of her existence, draws on knowledge, experience, and wisdom, and pours out unselfishly into the lives of others.

A much sought-after speaker, founder, and CEO of a network of companies and ministries, Dr. Trimm has traveled extensively throughout North and South America, Europe, the Caribbean, and Africa. Her unique style is permeated with intellectually compelling commentary, revolutionary insights, and contemporary practical applications.

She has received numerous honors and distinctions including awards from the Queen of England, the Duke of Edinburgh, and the Governor of Bermuda. Dr. Trimm is listed among the Five Hundred Leaders of Influence, 2000 Notable American Women, The International Who's Who of Professional and Business Women; receiving citations as Outstanding Christian Woman of the Year, Woman of the Year for Outstanding Community and Professional Achievement, and the 20th Century Award for Achievement.

A highly respected success coach and prosperity mentor to civic and spiritual leaders, indeed a leader of leaders, she emphatically states, "All these things that I once thought very worthwhile now I've cast aside so that I can put my trust and hope in Christ alone. Everything else is worthless when compared with the priceless gain in knowing Christ Jesus as my Lord."

For information on bookings or
to place an order:

Cindy Trimm Corporation
P.O. Box 101240
Ft. Lauderdale, FL 33311

www.cindytrimm.com

Phone: (954) 933-9191
Fax: (954) 934-0188
Email: www.cindytrimm.com